D1826517

Spiritual Journey

Claiming the Gifts in Pain and Suffering

A Healing Spiritual Journey--Volume V

JIM STACEY

Author of: Jesus Was Not a Christian
Discovering the Jesus Who was Replaced by Theology

meetjimstacey.com

When do we hide? From what do we hide? Why does it feel like hiding is the thing to do? Most of us have been told that we aren't "good enough", are "too small", need to "shut up and go away", need to "listen and obey" and other horrendous statements that come from those who are so filled with fear that they need to control us. There is no such reality as what we call "security." When we think we are most secure, are we really? When we think we are in danger, are we really? Sometimes outright exposure to what is fearful, is the best way to face it, overcome it, and transform it into a gift that takes us to a Higher Self. We never get anywhere by hiding. To what or whom will you say today, "I do not believe you any longer. I choose..."-- Jim Stacey

The most beautiful people we have known are those who have known pain, known defeat, known suffering, known struggle, known loss; and have found their way out of the depths of them all. These people have an appreciation, a sensitivity, and an understanding of life that fills them with compassion, gentleness, and a deep loving concern for others. Beautiful people do not just happen.-- Unknown

CONTENTS

A HEALING SPIRITUAL JOURNEY

This series of books, *A Healing Spiritual Journey,* is written not as a roadmap of spiritual directives, but rather as a guide to encourage you to make your own path of discovery and Divine connection. On a typical map you'll always find the easiest routes from _____ to _____. However, comparing a map that shows a whole country or a whole state on one page or two, is vastly different from the detailed local county map of the same areas.

Stretching across the landscape, at times so easy that it becomes a rather monotonous and tiresome means to reach a destination, the Interstate highway offers the fastest, most convenient, least bothersome way to travel. Racing past the unique energies of small towns, points of interest both historical and attractive to the curious mind, bypassing all but boredom, the superhighway is a vital piece of the "rat race" of a lost society, taking people quickly from nowhere to nowhere.

The secondary routes take more time, but you get a whole lot closer to what is along the way. The smallest lines on the map are always the slower ways to travel, yet they will take you to a connection with all you see rather than appearing as a blur out of your car window. The back roads of the country or the side streets of the city offer what the fastest route never can. Whether stopping to let some cows cross the road, pausing to look the homeless person in the eye with genuine compassion, talking to someone you've just met for the first time, creating more adventure as each new encounter with life opens possibilities and connections, the road least traveled offers far more than the road most traveled.

Then there are the trails for traveling on foot, hiking through a magnificent woods, sitting down to rest on a boulder that has been there for a few million years waiting for you, stumbling over that unseen piece of nature you didn't see because your attention was fixed on the beauty all around you, slipping here and there with a bit of glee in the midst of uncertainty, navigating a course around the trees or through them, and stopping to enjoy the cool shade they offer rather than the air-conditioned enclosure of your car. Streams, boulders, animals, trails, waterfalls, light and shadow all offer themselves as possibilities of adventure and delight. Without the "need" to hurry, hurry, hurry, which route would you choose? Where are you going so fast? Why is hurrying such a dis-ease? Is it the goal or the escape that drives you most? When have you last stopped to "smell the roses," take a deep breath and consciously disconnect with the distractions that demand your attention?

In this volume and the other 9 in this series, my attempt is to provide you with a "road less traveled" as Robert Frost wrote of in his poem.

The Road Not Taken.

Two roads diverged in a yellow wood,
And sorry I could not travel both
And be one traveler, long I stood
And looked down one as far as I could
To where it bent in the undergrowth;

Then took the other, as just as fair,
And having perhaps the better claim
Because it was grassy and wanted wear,
Though as for that the passing there
Had worn them really about the same,

And both that morning equally lay
In leaves no step had trodden back.
Oh, I marked the first for another day!
Yet knowing how way leads on to way
I doubted if I should ever come back.

I shall be telling this with a sigh,
Somewhere ages and ages hence:
Two roads diverged in a wood, and I,
I took the one less traveled by,
And that has made all the difference.

This insight from Robert Frost describes my own journey in so many ways. I have an original painting on my wall that beautifully depicts the scene in his poem. I've inscribed it with "Two Roads Diverged In A Yellow Wood..." The two roads, for me, was the road of the church and the road of the Aramaic Jesus. The church road was a theological superhighway from the "state" of a sinful world to the "state" of bliss in heaven. Jesus' road is the beauty of personal transformation that changes both the destination as well as the path of life we travel. I took the road less traveled...and that has made all the difference for me.

As I write this book for all who would dare choose their own path through the woods, I will point out some roads, some trails, some things to see and some to avoid, but the path you take **is your path!** Walk it with delight and expectancy to find your own Divinity, your purpose, your unique way to express your highest Self, and be who you've come here to be. Do you remember?

For many people, to follow the "path" that someone else made years ago probably seems to be the easiest way to get through the forest, but it certainly isn't the most adventurous, the most rewarding, or the most valuable. No one else's trail can be what meets your needs best. Many prefer the easy way because that seems to be the safest way to get through the woods. But is safety the only criterion for trailblazing? Let the fearful stay home and die on the porch if that feels best to them. I'll take the blazing of a new trail any day. Neither would I dare run through a forest blindfolded. That is sheer stupidity. I prefer to have my eyes wide open, be as prepared as possible for the journey, and then gain the experiences that can only come from blazing my own trail.

All that is well and good when talking about a physical trail through a real woods. This book is about finding a different kind of trail. When Emerson said: "Do not go where the path may lead, go instead where there is no path and leave a trail," he was speaking of two issues. The first is that of refusing to go only where others have gone and being satisfied with that. The second is that of blazing our own path and leaving behind us what is valuable for others who would learn from us and at the same time blaze their own trail. This is what I wish to accomplish with the message of these books.

The trail of others was never right for me. And, my life has been enriched by the hundreds of authors I've read, all the people I've known, friends, acquaintances, and even people I haven't liked (my temporary enemies). Yet there came a time for me to blaze my own trail, to take all of them with me, and to keep learning more and more. As I learn, I can share with others who will choose for themselves as they mark their own trail through life, finding themselves on their journey back home.

My wish for you is that you will gain much support from this book and the others in this series. I know you will. Then, I want to challenge you to go beyond where I've gone, learn more than anyone can teach you or share with you, and become a light for others to follow as they decide which trail to follow and when to move out on their own adventures.

I've written this ten volume series to offer assistance along your path to deeper spiritual discoveries, the following books hold some possibilities for your healing adventures to Divine connection in ways yet to be discovered and experienced deep within.

Volume I--The Divine Within: The Quest for Spiritual Identity

> Our spiritual identity is far more than religious labels! Humans have long labeled themselves out of convenience, pride, or a lack of knowing how to discover their own spiritual identity. Such labels as "Christian," "Buddhist," "Jewish," "Catholic," "Baptist," and a thousand others serve to confine and greatly restrict the human spirit to a very small place, as they deny the expression of their Sacred Self, and imprison them in their own backyard mud puddle. Within that narrow focus, the ocean of The Divine is never experienced. Join me on the Quest of many lifetimes! Your Divinity awaits you, for just

over the next mountain or around the next bend you will find...

Volume II--Spirituality: Experiencing the Divine Within

Sitting on a hard church pew, singing words about "God," throwing words of "worship" at "him," all while pretending to not be afraid of that angry, external Being, are the activities of those whose "God" is far too small. Theology and beliefs are but an effort to squeeze an elephant into a small doghouse, or the whole Universe into one's own backyard. Beliefs constrict the human spirit and rob us of our "birthright,"--the kingdom of heaven within, as Jesus taught. Divine connection expands our capacity to be, to love, to celebrate, to create beauty, to experience harmony, and to share life with other pilgrims on this journey we call life. There is much celebration ahead if you...

Volume III--Letting Go of All Illusions: The End of Guilt, Shame and Remorse

Beyond all the old feelings of shame, smallness, and worthlessness there is another perspective that changes everything. When is the last time you celebrated a mistake you made instead of feeling guilty? The Divine never condemns us--only men do that. Walk with me in the delights of hearing The Divine say: "All mistakes have their roots in Me." Our mistakes are NOT "sin." There are no opposites of wicked/righteous, guilty/innocent or even good/bad. The Divine sees us as much more than the labels of humanity. We are here on a path of learning from our mistakes, transforming our shadow parts, and choosing our highest Self on our way back Home. Let's dance together in the beauty of what we can only learn by making mistakes and growing beyond them. Your next choice is....

Volume IV--The Aramaic Jesus: The Message of the One Who LIVED for US

"When did 'God' become a woman?" I was asked one day. "When did 'God' become a man?" I replied. With a distinct look of dismay on his face, that minister had no answer for me. He had been sitting on his theological back porch for far too long to know of the amazing history of how humans have labeled The Divine out of their own very limited perspectives. Jesus knew the power of the Feminine face of The Divine and embodied Her as he healed, loved, showed compassion and empathy with those around him, and included everyone in the "family of The Divine." The Feminine knows about birthing and is an immeasurable help in birthing a new Self as Jesus required of all who would know of his call to "birth a new self" continuously. Your most magnificent Self is awaiting your response to Her. The power you will know deep inside is the power to...

Volume V--The Spiritual Journey: Claiming the Gifts in Pain and Suffering

Picking raspberries or blackberries results in the scrumptious, mouth pleasing flavors that bring delightful celebration to the palate as those sweet, juicy berries are crushed in ones mouth and yield their flavors to be enjoyed. At the same time, we know going into the briar patch that there will likely be some pain experienced from the very sharp thorns that surround those morsels we treasure. So why do we knowingly risk the scrapes, scratches, or punctures of the skin, as well as the ticks, the bees, and the mosquitoes? Why do we live life knowing that pain and suffering are going to be our companions at times? Yet pain and suffering can bring to us greater treasures than we can imagine, a life purpose yet unknown, and reasons to celebrate our being here for this lifetime. What are the treasures that last forever? Your inner treasure awaits your claiming the...

Volume VI--Entering What is Already Within: The Kingdom/Queendom In Balance

How does one **enter** that which is already **within** them? This is the grand question that the church has never answered because their theology can't handle it. Jesus taught, "The Kingdom of heaven is within you" as the most important spiritual reality. Then his whole life's teachings were about "entering the Kingdom." He told the religious ones that the "harlots and the tax collectors will enter it before you do, that the rich will have great difficulty entering it if at all, and that until we "become as little children" we will never enter it. That Kingdom has zero to do with any form of government. That is only a human projection. The Divine does not govern. Yet "entering" is required if we are to know our deepest purpose for being here. And, your first step is...

Volume VII--Men as the Weaker Sex: Controlling Others with Fear, Guilt and Shame

Who is strongest--the one who can lift 300 pounds, or the one who knows that the "need" to compete with others isn't necessary? To prove what cannot be proven is the quest of the shadow masculine out of a focus on his own insecurities and his need to convince others that he is "right" by speaking loudly, making rules for others, competing, and winning (whatever "winning" means). Above all, he needs to control others by any means possible. The control-oriented male is the weaker sex. When is a man tough enough to love? To serve? To heal? To choose compassion over competition? Too many men need to lie in order to gain control over others. Join me on an adventure of breaking free from the lies of the religious patriarchs--the lies of organized Christianity and the agonizing restrictions it has put upon all people. The Christian Church has sinned! It is their turn to repent. From the "95" sins of the church listed in this book, to the utter failure of fabricated beliefs, its horrific failure to love others as Jesus taught, its ignorance of what he required, its blind choices to not practice his words, and its abject refusal to care for a world steeped in blindness, Christianity has failed! Beyond the teachings of Jesus, that it ignores, Christianity has become the greatest source of the wounding of the human spirit where a "sin" focus is more valuable than love. Learn how to free yourself from the wounds of shame, guilt, judgments, blame, and condemnation that twist the human soul rather than set it free. The real God isn't angry with us. The church has been lying about that for over 1700 years.

Volume VIII--Conversations with "St." Paul, The Homophobic Preacher: Owning Our Shadows and Healing Deep Within

There is a fly in the ointment! Something's rotten in Denmark! There's a cockroach in your beer! Statements about the inherent flaw than can be found in almost anything are common. What is the shadow that was built into Christianity from the very beginning? Who did it? Why? You'll laugh with me, on this adventure as we learn the truth about Paul, the real founder of Christianity. Being trapped in fear and the condemnation of the self-righteous is not the doorway to your Divinity. May you experience great freedom to be fully who you are and celebrate that transformation as you read this and take it deep inside yourself. Since our sexuality is part of our Divinity, we cannot "sin" by being sexual! And, we must avoid using sex to hurt another person. Come with me, on this adventure as we learn the truth about Paul, the real founder of the Christian faith. Discover a Paul who never once quoted Jesus. He never taught one principle that was vital to Jesus' teachings. Being trapped in fear and the condemnation of the self-righteous is not the doorway to your Divinity. May you experience great freedom to be fully who you are and celebrate that transformation as you read this and take it deep inside yourself. Healing is afoot!

Volume IX--Creating Intimate Relationships: The Secret of Shared Divinity

Do relationships just happen? Or are they the results of something not quite that easy? We all have relationships--some meaningful, some delightful, some more functional, or just necessary. Yet why are some difficult and challenging, dysfunctional and frustrating? All authentic and conscious relationships are the results of practicing some very important principles. I must be authentic before I can expect anyone else to be that. I must seek relationships, not just to get my needs met. Unless I am committed to being one who helps others get their needs met, I am woefully lacking in what is required to create and build intimacy wherein everyone is honored. All of our old "stuff" shows up in relationships. What I am willing to do about that will determine how successful I am in creating relationships that heal and grow into great delight.

Volume X--Sacred Parenting: Raising Unexpected Divinity

Brats, rug rats or a Divine commission? Why did you become a parent? How easy it is to lose sight of one of the most important contributions you can make to the planet by choosing to be parents. From the dirty diapers, the "terrible twos," teen rebellion, and all the other episodes of raising children; unless we see **that greater gift** in parenting we can sometimes lose the greater insight. But now you can see that more clearly than ever as you reclaim your greatest gift--your children and their contributions to life. Seeing your children as Divine Beings here under your care makes all the difference. The more parents see themselves as Divine Beings, the easier it will be to see The Divine in them. See Vol. I and II of this series and you can begin your adventure anew.

Discovering "Truth" is never a destination--it is the ongoing adventure of our lifetimes! Bless you on your path!

Preface

It is the best of times, it is the worst of times, the delights of being human, as well as the death-wish in our deepest secret self; the human drama we both carry within our hearts and upon our backs. The gifts we open along our journey, the paradox of life itself, adding celebration to our inner abundance, feeling heartbreak bring to us an anguish that tempers the soul wholly focused on pleasure, opening the doors of magic and wonder, shutting down the hopes and dreams we've long cherished, life unfolds and faces us with the deepest choices of our existence. How shall I live this one lifetime?

The ways in which I lived my last lifetime and just how I will live the next one are both beyond the consciousness of today. This moment in this lifetime is all that I have. How will I use this moment to create the unimaginable, assemble the pieces of the puzzle that seem to not fit together at all, to harvest the treasure that has so long seemed out of reach?

Join me as we walk the path of a spiritual journey on which you will claim all of these and more. Your journey is vastly more beautiful than you've known, for you are now about to claim the greatest treasure you'll ever know.

We have all experienced the **delights** of being alive, the **rewards** for hard work, the **serendipity** of circumstances coming together in ways more magical than we could have planned ourselves, **relationships unfolding** into loving connections before unknown to us, and **possibilities opening** before us that we couldn't see yesterday.

Then there's the death-wish that has haunted us in our deepest secret self, the fears that have gripped our soul, the pain we thought we'd never endure, the torment of losses that we felt we so desperately needed, the apparent failures that have frustrated us and have tempted us to think of ourselves as being far too small, and the loss of relationships we'd hoped would endure.

Suddenly in the midst of pain and suffering a new dawn breaks upon the landscape of our souls, a Source of light, healing and hope--an awareness that all of our experiences hold Divine purpose, the becoming of a new self and a stepping into a deeper reason for being here on the planet than we've ever known. Suddenly we are becoming more alive than ever before.

What is that dawning of a new day? How do we see it? What is the inner realization that comes to us as an open door through which we now can step through to claim our unique path? That dawning begins to break upon our horizon when we, in the midst of one more sunrise of struggle, ask: Why this again?

An interesting insight is revealed in the following poem from Rumi.

Boil Nicely Now

Look at the chickpea in the pot,
how it leaps up when it feels the fire.
While boiling, it continually rises to the top and cries,
"Why are you setting the fire under me?
Since you bought me, why are you turning me upside down?"
The housewife keeps hitting it with the ladle.
"No!" she says, "boil nicely now,
and don't leap away from the one who makes the fire.
It's not because you are hateful to me that I boil you,
but so that you might gain flavor,
and become nutritious and mingle with essential spirit.
This affliction is not because you are despised.
When you were green and fresh,
you were drinking water in the garden;
that water-drinking was for the sake of this fire."—
Rumi

So often we do as we have been taught and see pain or difficulties as some sort of punishment. We've been taught to see them this way. But, The Divine is not ever punishing us--only allowing us to be developed into a sweetness that will bring healing to others.

INTRODUCTION

It is the unanswered question for most of humanity. It is the place that holds our deepest fears. It is the scene we most want to avoid. The mind shuts off any thought of pursuing it. The heart feels faint at the very slightest mention of it. The strongest of men only shout louder to try to drown out their fear of looking into it. The weakest of men can only feel they are victims of it.

What is this fear and dilemma all about? How can anything have so much power over the human? For beyond its prison, living in slavery to it, or the smallest box of one's beliefs is the courage to not just ask that question, but to awaken to find the answer. That question is: **Why is there so much pain and suffering in the human experience?**

Many have tried to write about this question. Many have failed to answer it. The "problem of pain" seems to be the unanswerable question for so many. But why? Theology has no answer. Religion has no answer. Philosophy has no answer. It seems that the "why" of the "pain problem" escapes into the recesses of the soul that only knows separation, guilt, shame, and fear of punishment. It is mostly an unanswerable question, until--

until, that is, we discover the insights that are beyond the Western mindset.

Do we choose pain and suffering, or do they choose us? Why is pain and suffering the universal experience of all humanity? Even the billionaire who can buy anything he wants, cannot prevent pain and suffering from coming his way nor does his money alleviate the pain when it does come. Yet is this not the biggest issue behind greed? But the more one possesses of the physical world, the more it seems that they are desperately trying to use their possessions to somehow try to avoid pain and suffering. No one can build a portfolio large enough that it will not be shaken.

But such is the delusion of every human that has not yet discovered the gifts to be found in pain and suffering. Is not a part of all pain and suffering, the fact that we have put too much stock into things that are temporary at best? Those who allow themselves to become deeply attached to the temporary, find themselves in a constant state of vulnerability and victim energy because they cannot control their own fate. Then, when pain and suffering arrive, instead of choosing the spiritual practice of claiming the gifts therein, men often cry in secret.

Hiding just behind the pain of the roses thorns, the sting of the bees, the weeds that torment, blisters on fingers, aching joints and sore knees, sweat on the brow, and swelling that lingers, the beauty and aroma of roses beckons me to come, enter, embrace and experience the gifts they offer.

As the most magnificent rose garden you thought you could never leave, brings to your memory splendid light falling softly upon the rose petals, their fragrances mystifying the mind but well know to your soul, a succulent radiance opening your memory, and the awareness that there is always more beauty awaiting you on your journey, you merge into the enveloping magnificence knowing that you and Beauty are One.

Beyond our humanity and the thorns of the human experience another awareness beckons us to come and experience beauty where we thought it could never be found, delight where we were certain it was not, and a deep purpose we've doubted we'd ever discover.

Such is the spiritual path of the human who has come to the planet, having temporarily laid aside all past experiences, here to learn more, become more and to remember why we agreed to come into human form once again. We are not here to remember the details of past experiences but to remember who we are. We are here to awaken from all that has kept us in bondage, to choose to continually search for deeper truths, to recognize the beauty of our shadow self, to learn of the magnificence in the transformation of it, to claim our true Self--our DIVINITY, and to step into a greater, more fulfilling purpose than we have thought possible. We must learn to see beyond all that clutters our vision with all that is temporary and passing away. The dualism of Western thinking is a trap that keeps people in a very small and difficult place. I love what Rumi says about this:

> "Out beyond ideas of wrongdoing and right-doing, there is a field. I'll meet you there."--Rumi

CHAPTER 1--REFUSING TO WAKE UP

We all need wake-up calls at times. Life can become so busy, stressful, and pressing that we find ourselves living patterns of behavior that seem to work most of the time and then--another loss, another wall, another hurdle, another reason to lose hope. But if our eyes are closed or we are asleep, we tend to label the world as "terrible" or "unfair" or whatever allows us to keep pretending. However, when the eyes are opened to the wisdom of spiritual depths beyond beliefs, we can not only see the issue differently, but we can transform it into a gift that sets us free. To know deep inside that our "self" never had a beginning like the body did. The "self" was never born nor will it ever perish or cease to exist. Never! You are not only "birth-less" but you are part of the eternal living beauty of the Universe. There is hope!

Every issue deep within that we've pushed aside, hoped it had finally gone away, or ignored because it is someone else's fault, **will always return,** and return again until we choose to embrace it, learn from it, transform the negative into light for our path and walk free from it-- finally! Then, thankfully, there will be more to learn and a higher consciousness to attain.

Nothing of value in this life will ever be claimed and owned by force or by anger. Those energies only push issues away and as I try to exclude myself from being part of the solution. Blaming someone else will neither make me a better person nor relieve me from responsibility for the issue at hand. The more I push issues away, the more I find myself standing alone. But recognizing and dealing with the "alone factor" can help me recognize my shadow self if I begin to own my shadow in every issue. There is nothing like "alone" to bring out self-justification, anger, blame, guilt, manipulation, self-righteousness, the desire to control all others around me. In that false feeling of safety I somehow try to figure out why people are keeping their distance from me. The person I choose to exclude is likely to be the key to my healing. They are only a mirror reflecting back to me what I desperately tried to push away. Subconsciously I push that person away because I don't want to admit that I have something to learn and transform. That person is only me showing my issues back to myself in that moment of rejection. Which "me" is the real one?

Other people are not here to be controlled. You are not here to be controlled. WE are all here to be included, celebrated, and honored as parts of each others' journey back home. Control comes at us from those who feel very small; so small that they use others to desperately try to overcome their smallness. Making others small by controlling them only feeds our smallness. We reap what we have sown. Some of the ways we try to make each other small is by using anger, judgments, shame, blame, rules, a self-righteousness that wants to push guilt away. Our "need" to be right overcomes a sense of honesty! **To exclude others is to refuse healing for ourselves.**

But who has taught us to exclude others and push them away? Society? Culture? Yes, but what is the source of the values or lack thereof which have shaped the mindset of the people? The answer is very clear. The source of all separation, exclusion, self-righteousness, racism, hatred masked with "faith" and the extreme "need" to feel better than others is found in one word-- BELIEFS! Beliefs are one's greatest enemy--one's prison of shame and smallness. Beliefs constrict the soul, the mind and the heart as the "believers" work so hard to feel they possess the truth! They do not!

Consider the image of the believer who, in his desperate search to feel that he possesses the truth, finds a small box, puts his beliefs into it, seals it tightly, defends it with no small amount of fear, and then condemns all others whose box has different contents than his. The "need" to feel that one possesses the truth is the curse of all belief systems. A sailor whose ship is tightly anchored in the bay is not safer in the long run than the sailor out on the high seas navigating, exploring, learning, plunging and rising as he gains wisdom that he cannot ever know by just pretending to be a sailor. A sailor only needs an anchor when he is not sailing. A man only needs beliefs when he is not truly living.

Those with small boxes are the ones who "need" to fight, compete, control, overcome, cheat, lie, and excuse all of that because he desperately needs to think that he is the one with the "truth." Beliefs exclude others. Growing and learning include others. Beliefs are like the story *The Emperor Has No Clothes!* In that story the naked emperor was pretending to be what he was not until a small boy shouted out the truth of what he saw. Including all others in the community of humanity is to remember who we are, to be conscious and content in our not knowing all the truth--but are always awakening to more.

There is no gift quite as valuable as the gift that awakens us to higher consciousness--the gift that rips open the box of beliefs and sets us free. Pain and suffering are exactly that when we allow it to be that catalyst. That gift many times is found in the experience of pain and suffering. We can learn to exchange all the old beliefs and their baggage of unconsciousness and actually learn from pain and suffering instead of pretending that all we need is our little box of beliefs.

Below are two lists. One is the elements of consciousness and the other the characteristics of just beliefs only. Everything in the beliefs column can be exchanged for what is in the consciousness column. But how? The practice of claiming the gifts in pain and suffering is unfolded in the pages ahead. But it all begins with the choice to wake up. Then there is a lifetime of choices just ahead as we choose to live in the energies of our highest Self.

Consciousness	Beliefs
Awareness	Doubt
Intuition	Ego
Openness	Arguing
Desire	Disowned Self
Willingness	Limitations
Living the Truth	Beliefs only
Not giving up	Excuses
What I must do	What you must do
Connection with	Strife and conflict
Doing, taking action	Languishing in excuses
Peacemaking	War
Loving	Abusing
Delight	Excuses to be upset
Peace	Chaos
Getting real needs met	Rejection
Accomplishment	Stalemate
Divine connection	Not good enough
Self-esteem	Self-loathing
Boundaries	No validation of self

| Choice to be more | Limited to beliefs only |
| Adventure | Slippery Slope of torment |

Saying there are gifts in pain/suffering is not to ask for more suffering just so you can get some more gifts. To say that is, rather, a declaration that opens the door for a deeper understanding and an immense possibility that has here-to-fore escaped the radar screen of the unconscious mind. Pain and suffering are neither accidental nor deserved, but rather your key to awakening from the deceptions, the false comforts, and the misconceptions that you should be able to live here pain free. You've come here to learn what "being" is all about. The false notion that the more money one has to buy the comforts and experiences that will keep you from the pain and suffering experiences, is sheer folly. Instead of clinging desperately to what is only a fleeting experience, you can learn to remember why you are here. Do you want to remember?

CHAPTER 2--THE ONGOING REALITY OF BEING

Walking alongside a delightful wooded creek in upper Michigan, my awareness of the nature of that stream opened to the mystical wonder of all that was before me in that moment. As I pondered the beauty of the flowing water, I experienced a penetrating insight into the "stream" that we call life. That enticing stream had never before been exactly as I was seeing it that day. None of the drops of water that came together to form that stream in this moment had ever been together in exactly the same way before, and I knew that never again would anyone see exactly what I was seeing at that point in time.

Since water can never be destroyed, I wondered just where each drop might have been since the time the earth came into form when Creator called forth light from the face of the deep. What was it like to be part of this beautiful stream compared to having been a drop in the ocean, a mighty river, ice at the South Pole, mist in a cloud, a droplet of morning dew on a rose petal, or as steam coming out of my morning cup of cappuccino. The water in that stream had been all over the planet, I mused, and its journey was not to end in this place either. Its journey today was but a continuum on the eternal path of all that is part of The Divine. Each drop had a journey ahead that was, as yet, unknown. In that unknown dimension lies both the mystery and the delights of this present adventure that we call existence.

Our lives are, in many ways, like a drop of water in a stream. Where have we been in our past experiences that are beyond our memories? Where will we yet be in the unfolding present? To where shall we roam as a being that is yet to become all that we choose in the days ahead. These are but the unanswerable ponderings in this existential reality that we call "life."

Of all the possibilities downstream, what experiences would each drop of that water realize—the next bend, the waterfall just ahead, the river only a few miles away--the ocean? A myriad of possible adventures are awaiting each drop as it flows, widens into a quiet pool, falls over rocks and branches, or breaks into a fast moving current along the way. Will it be caught by a thirsty plant, a tree, a butterfly, a raccoon, or a deer? Perhaps, for a time, it will be part of a brain cell in the deer or maybe pass through its digestive system and temporarily be part of some waste on the ground. Sometimes in life it seems that this has happened to us, but that is only temporary. Each drop of water will surely evaporate and return to the atmosphere above. Or will it be carried away on the feet of a crane that has been feeding in the waters? What then is its path to be? Will it be splashed upon a rock or fallen tree, evaporate into the air, help form a cloud, and once again ride the winds until it falls as rain somewhere else on the surface of the planet? At that moment, it will be on another unknown adventure of sustaining life anew.

Each drop of water, like the human spirit, can never be trapped forever. It will not fail to fulfill its purpose— and neither will you. For sure, there will be times of waiting and wondering why all the present circumstances are happening; times when you will feel like you're are stuck in a hidden place without seeming to have much hope. But, emerge you will, just as the drop of water, and your journey will continue with greater wisdom than you had before the experience just realized. Beyond right/wrong, beyond good/bad and other human judgments, we are part of all that is. We are One with each other and The Divine. We cannot be lost!

There were times when my life seemed like a drop of water that had surely lost its way. The trauma of a painful childhood was too much to bear, yet I could not escape the torment—at least until later in life. Raised and abused in the midst of fundamentalist Christianity, there was nothing in traditional Christianity that provided answers for my inner pain. I was raised to feel a shame which only served to exacerbate my grief as a wounded child. The inner "victim" would not be silenced. I came to the understanding that theology has no power to heal.

Only love and divine connection through spiritual practices can heal the human spirit.

And, no human soul can or will be lost in pain and suffering either. We are here to learn through the experiences of pain and suffering--not to give in to them and feel that victim energy. As Gandhi said: "First they ignore you, then they laugh at you, then they fight you, then you win." But it is only when we get past the victim stages of misunderstanding pain and suffering, that we can WIN! But what does it mean to win? Winning does not mean that someone else has to lose. That is Western thinking.

How many times have we "caught" ourselves thinking that pain is evil and pleasure is good. Is pain "evil" because it is uncomfortable or disturbing? Perhaps what most humans hold unconsciously is the constant battle between what they perceive as good or evil. To see "good and evil," however, does not represent consciousness in any way whatsoever. Our quest must be for what is beyond good and evil; beyond pleasure and what feels bad mentally, emotionally, or physically. Of course it is always in our best interest to eschew "evil" and turn from that energy. But is it enough to focus on "good?" Just what is evil? What is that which we label as good? Why do we engage ourselves in this ongoing wrestling match to define these? Is pain/suffering just an experience of "evil" or is there more? Is being pain free and unconsciously experiencing the false pleasures of the material world what we define as "good" or are we aware yet, that material things do not ultimately satisfy? Why have temporary experiences of what we label as good or evil become so important that we forget what is beyond both. All that we can know beyond good and evil is what this book is about.

What does that "beyond" look like for you? Are you like that drop of water in the stream that flows beyond all obstacles where you find yourself thriving because of the gifts you discovered in what was painful instead of being defeated by them? Have you ever felt gratitude for a painful experience that taught you a powerful lesson and helped make your life more beautiful? You can know this personally and live in gratitude without the old barriers to celebrating your journey.

CHAPTER 3--REDEFINING LIFE'S EVENTS

The experience of flying is much like our experience of living wherein the constant adjustments due to the air currents, weather, and the "control tower" are the norm. The admixture of voices from flight control and the pilots own experience in the cockpit must be integrated if the experience of flying, taking off, and landing is to be successful. All of those adjustments begin immediately as the aircraft starts down the runway and don't end until after touchdown. It has been said that flying is the second greatest thrill for humans. The greatest thrill is landing. Sometimes our greatest thrill is to overcome pain and suffering.

Perhaps our lives and the adventures within it are like many take offs and landings. On one such adventure, many years ago, rising and falling through the air currents much like the worst roller coaster I could imagine, holding my breath in the tense moments of uncertainty, gripping my seat with no small amount of fear, wishing with much emotion that I'd never taken this flight, feeling sickness in my stomach, my head aching from the stress of what felt like great danger, seeing the faces of other terrified passengers, hearing the sounds of tension, fear, dismay and more, wondering if this trauma would ever end as the plane plunged, darted about, climbed again, fluttered through the air currents, bounced along the pockets of turbulent air, only to repeat all this over and over again but then to finally smooth out, safely landing to everyone's extreme relief and delight; except the man across from me who, unknowingly to us all, had died of a heart attack only moments before.

Life's adventures are but a myriad of experiences; each one lived by us wherein many times we find ourselves alone and faced with the need to choose our way through. Life is choices. In many ways our entire life is but a series of choices moment by moment, hour by hour, one lifetime at a time. What choices we make, what patterns we develop, what differences we experience, what memories we hold, what pain we have been through, what disowned parts of our self we've hidden, what suffering we've endured, what moments of sheer delight come our way, what fears we never talk about, what moments of celebration have been ours, we are constantly choosing in order to experience one goal and one goal only. That goal is the same for you, for me and for every other person on the planet. That goal is the get our "needs" met, wherein we don't always make the best choices, yet they are our choices designed to get us to some place, to land safely, to experience life, and to learn in that process just what our "needs" really are.

We all need self-worth, purpose, choice integrity, connection, inclusion, appreciation, respect, community, mutual trust, love, safety, celebration, beauty harmony and sharing of both grief and triumph and much more. Consciously or not, we are doing our best to get our needs met. The ways in which we meet them are not always in our best interest, it seems, and certainly not in the best interests of others at times. In the process of living, our mistakes are not the evidence of something "bad!" Our mistakes can be, if we are to celebrate life in any deep way at all, that which can reveal to us what is possible to be and become. We always grow from _____ to _____, or we take another "flight" from _____ to _____. The beauty within our existence as humans is that we are never trapped in this moment. We can always choose our way out, however difficult or easy those choices and the results of each may be.

> "The difference between your mistakes and the mistakes of enlightened Beings rests in their ability to practice true forgiveness. They realize that if the mistakes of others should be forgiven immediately, then so should theirs...most carry their mistakes and their guilt with them for eons, but   there is no need for that." (*The Disappearance of the Universe,* Renard, p. 63)

We can never break loose from our mistakes until we realize just what chains are binding us and keeping us in prison. What if the pilot never listened to the control tower? What if he/she totally took "control" from the cockpit, turned the radio off and flew by "the seat of their pants"? I'm sure no pilot has logged enough flight hours to get through the next "flight from hell." A good pilot always needs someone with a greater perspective, a different perspective, and a larger overview.

This is much like our inner life experiences. Do I depend on myself or do I learn to trust a higher guidance? How do I know the difference? Do we know ourselves as human only, or as both human and Divine? The Aramaic Jesus spoke of this issue when he said "The Greater I AM is within the smaller I am." He revealed that knowing the experience of that truth is the way back to The Divine, the right direction on that path and the strength to walk that path all the way home. (For details on this see my book, *Jesus Was Not A Christian,* on Amazon) The truth is that we are Divine in the midst of having a human experience we call life--the school for learning all that can take us to the place of greater service in the eternal purposes of The Universe that we have temporarily forgotten.

For some, however, to listen to the "still small voice" within, the voice of The Divine that is available to us constantly, is but an idea to be scoffed at and disowned. "You're nuts" is a common response to the idea that one can actually learn to "hear" an inaudible, silent voice within! Yet, we are highly experienced at listening to the inaudible voice of the ego that dictates our behavior much more than most of us are willing to admit at times. The ego says (silently) "yell at that idiot," "put that person down," "isn't he stupid?," "repeat a story about her," "look down upon him," "you're so much more enlightened that she is," "he is guilty, not you," and so many more projections and judgments that come directly out of our ego, while all the time the ego doesn't want us to see that it is in control. We are so used to hearing the silent voice of the ego, yet we don't make enough effort to learn to listen to the silent voice of The Divine within. What else could an awakened intuition be? Then there are those who think they're listening to The Divine and they always tell others what to do or in some ego way have become "Divine experts" in their own minds--the dark side of some "new age" thinking or the darkness of religion. The ego never wants to see "gifts" in pain and suffering. It would rather use all pain or suffering to serve itself by blaming others for these experiences.

The crucial issue for the human is to be able to "hear" The Divine and practice the loving principles that always come from the Source of Love. This requires: **first,** the desire to "hear" beyond the ego, **second,** the courage to do the inner transformative work that is required so one can begin to "hear," and **third,** the choice to ask for the ears to hear, the heart to understand and the courage to follow through and practice what one then hears is needed. The ego doesn't want us to "hear" the other voice, to pay attention to it, to practice loving principles or anything else that puts blame on one's shadow instead of blaming others, projecting our stuff onto them, holding them guilty, and using them as an external scapegoat for our own failings. Right in the middle of scapEGOat we find the real problem. The ego loves projections and judgments. Those are its means of staying hidden beneath the shadows and holding onto its own garbage. These choices are our biggest mistakes.

The luxury of holding others guilty is that we never have to look within. The false sense of being better than others is but the trap of the ego for its own protection. As long as I have him to blame for _____ and her to hold accountable for _____, I can continue in a self-justification that loves to hide behind grudges and battles with those who I love to dislike.

Forgiveness? "Who needs that?" asks the ego. Yet, the ego knows that if I forgive others, then I no longer have someone external to myself to blame and then use as an excuse to hide my own stuff. "...those who hold grievances will suffer guilt, as it is certain that those who forgive will find peace...those who hold grievances will forget who they are, as it is certain that those who forgive will remember." (Ibid. p. 158) We come up against things that we don't want to give up. "That's how your resistance and your hidden, unconscious hatred shows up. Those are the things you're going to have to look at." (Ibid. p. 159) "...real peace is found by undoing the ego, not by covering it over." (p. 160)

So what is it about our "ego" mistakes that can bring us to celebration? Once we begin to disarm the ego, we can begin to see our true selves. There is no greater gift than that. When we begin the transformation of the old pain, guilt, suffering from the past and rid our minds of the ghosts from our past, only then can we begin to claim our Divinity--the kingdom of heaven within. A mistake that leads us to learning a valuable insight is cause for celebration.

To celebrate in the midst of our mistakes and learn from them is but the evidence of an enrichment that comes to us from learning how to live in "the question" rather than fooling ourselves by hiding in our shadows. In this experience is the magic of serendipity. Once we discover the hidden gifts that we can find in pain and suffering, our life changes dramatically because as we begin to know more of our life purpose that is beyond the smallness of the temporary world.

The transformed self is cause for both great celebration and stepping into empathy, healing, and loving others along our path. There is nothing quite as powerful as when one who has been wounded, does their inner work and then becomes the "wounded healer" for others. Now that, is worth celebrating!

CHAPTER 4--ATTACHMENTS--HOLDING ONTO PAIN

Remember the last time you felt pain from the thorns of a raspberry bush   as you picked some delicious morsels to eat? Remember the times you've felt the thorns of a rose when smelling its delightful fragrance? The sting of thorns can be a painful experience if the puncture of the skin is prolonged. When feeling the pain of those thorns, why didn't you squeeze them even harder? A bizarre question? Yes, but that is exactly what we do so often with painful situations in our lives-- we hold onto them or even hold them tighter out of the fear of letting go! But why would we ever hold onto pain instead of letting go of it?

The truth is that so many people hold onto what is painful and keep enduring the pain because pain is so familiar. All that is familiar is preferable over what is unknown because one fears what is not certain. It is easier to hold onto familiar pain than it is to let it (or that person or circumstance) go and take a chance that change might be better! Many times fear is the reason we hold onto pain and suffering. In that fear we become attached to our pain and trapped in suffering.

We choose our attachments because they feel like "safety" for the soul that dwells in fear. Actually, they only increase the "danger" of not becoming all we are destined to be. The soul that has never known freedom, falsely sees the trap of temporary attachments as the "freedom" it seeks, instead of the adventures beyond what is comfortable that can take us to heights otherwise unattainable.

You are attached to pain and suffering when you keep making excuses for it instead of finding out how to let it go. Accusing others for causing your pain is only trying desperately to avoid taking responsibility for what is **your pain!** To accuse others of violating your boundaries instead of "showing them the door" is to harm oneself. But to drop a bomb of accusations onto another person and then run away is just another act of irresponsibility. You can play the games of blame if you like, but why not take responsibility for the pain and suffering you've experienced and change your life? Oh, I forgot--is fear the reason you cannot do that? Hmmm...

Fear is almost always present when 1) you allow pain and suffering to be part of your identity, 2) you hold onto pain as an excuse to live with anger, 3) you justify your reactions, criticism of others, resentments and projections, 4) you see others issues more than your own, 5) you refuse to see others as your own image in the mirror of life, 6) you cannot seem to attract love into your life, 7) you are focused on getting your way, 8) you care not about the needs of others, 9) you use pleasure as a substitute for personal change, 10) you absolutely must convince others that you are "right" and they are wrong, 11) you refuse to genuinely listen to others and their issues, 12) you unconsciously feel that suffering is part of your identity, and 13) you think you deserve the pain and suffering that you know so well. Fear is a big part of all these. When will we come to know that pain and suffering is not our birthright nor does it need to be an unwanted companion on our life journey?

When Prayer Does Not Work

It is much easier to just "pray about" pain and suffering than it is to recognize that you might be habitually clinging to unconsciousness and fear. Prayer is easier than doing the inner work required to live beyond pain and suffering. Prayer, many times, is only an excuse to repeat all your actions and choices that got you into that pain and suffering in the first place. Prayer can be the refusal to live responsibly in the creative place of uncertainty and choosing your way out of where you don't want to be any longer.

Prayer cannot heal! Why? Because prayer so often is nothing but bargaining with some deity who you believe is somehow the answer to living pain free. But no "god" is responsible for that--you are! Prayer is many times like a vending machine into which you put your coins of confession, remorse, penitence, shame, guilt, and bargaining in order to somehow merit an "answer" that will get you out of the mess you're in. Then when that answer does not come out as desired, you kick the machine with more begging until it does. Kicking the machine in those ways is only more self-abuse because of the inherent belief that you do not deserve an answer.

Prayer is usually a focus on the current problems. Prayer can be just a form of bondage to the problem instead of a release from it. Instead of wanting to see what is blocking your receiving some answer and choosing to remove the blocks, perhaps you only want things to change without changing yourself. Change your beliefs and change who you become.

The old church excuse for staying in pain and suffering is what I heard in the church long ago. "Give your problems to the lord" was the old adage of the sufferers. But whoever your "lord" is, "he" does not want your problems, neither is that "lord" responsible for the choices that you or others made in getting into them. You alone are responsible for changing. And, you alone can choose your path to seeing the hidden gifts awaiting your choices to be authentic, responsible, and creative. Using prayer to focus on a problem will only bind you to the problem even more instead of releasing it through more conscious choices and rising above it. Real prayer is a focus on personal responsibility for the problem and the choices to change the belief patterns that created it in the first place. Real prayer is never asking! It is opening to what is new and creative. The only "prayer" we ever need is "Thank You" for showing me what is hindering we from receiving what I need.

Real prayer is opening to the conscious choices that will set you free because you choose to own your issues, take responsibility for them, and then choose to change whatever is required. That requires courage! The courage to face the unknown, open to all possibilities, make new choices, test those choices and choose again and again. We learn the most from our choices and the results of them. Then we get to apply what we learn and make better choices than we've made before. **The choice to change is never ending!** The conservative mindset will usually stay stuck in fear. The spiritual pilgrim will always be looking for the next road to take to freedom, responsibility and love. The Aramaic sense of prayer is seen in the teachings of Yeshua. He taught that "prayer" is not asking for something, but rather the "emptying" of what is blocking us from receiving what we need. To become aware of the blocks, we can then remove them by choosing to live differently. We can live in expectation and delight instead of shame and lack.

Real prayer is about changing you--not changing someone else! So often the ego wants to change others so they'll be more like you and then you'll be more comfortable. The ego refuses to see that others' differences are present and that because of them you will be challenged to keep learning and growing. Your ego wants to change others by pressuring them and even trying to force them to be what you want instead of changing yourself by including others and learning from them.

Prayer, as normally understood, is but the tool of religions to keep people under control. Prayer is the by-product of a religion that teaches people that they deserve to be victims of pain and suffering. Prayer becomes a religious way of coping with life under the shame and blame that religions teach. Religion keeps people bound up in the temporary three-dimensional world that is not reality anymore than religion itself is. Religion is just a part of what is passing away. It is no wonder that religious people are attached to pain and suffering--they believe they deserve it until some future paradise is attained. But a religious "heaven" can wait! You can know the beauty of choosing your way out or religious bondage into the delights of being free from dogma. You deserve to be your real Self--The Divine Within as the real Jesus taught. (See Volumes I, II, and IV of this series)

Fear keeps people imprisoned in "sin" (the fabricated idea of the church) instead of gaining the spiritual insights that will set them free. Fear is control instead of choosing for yourself. Fear is hiding and pretending instead of learning on your own "slippery slope" as does a downhill skier. We must understand that we have more than one "self."

> "That is why we have to move away from the level of behaviourism. We cannot deny the "self." But we must understand that there is a self" that solely relates to the world, and another, higher "Self' which is without limitations and in perfect balance with all the aspects of life. While the little "self" is busy counting its money and planning the future, creating strategies and nurturing its career, shopping and consuming, worrying and looking for confirmation, the higher "Self" is simply concerned with being. While the little "self" feels that it needs all its activities in order to function, the higher "Self" is because it is totally free of any excess luggage." p. 54, The "O" Manuscript, by Lars Muhl.

To choose to let go of fear-motivated attachments is the first step. These are only part of our "lower self" (ego). So often we become depressed because we are focused on ourselves and our problems. This focus is our most self-centered state of being.

> "If we only relate to this level of behaviour, we soon find that everything we seek is based on fear. As long as we remain at this level and refuse to

see that there are other levels, we shall basically
think and act from fear for the rest of our lives."
Ibid.

Religion is many times just the ideology of
limitations. Spirituality is embracing what we heretofore
have pushed away--our Higher Self--The Divine within us
(See www.thedivineiswithinus.com for details), and all the
sheer beauty of your personal adventure.

Living In The Mystery

The mystery is not a clinging to the illusions of
religion. The mystery is the adventure of choosing your
own spiritual path that opens you to the Beauty of The
Divine within you and all that this means. Theology closes
us down. Spirituality opens us to the mystery of Divine
encounters. Religion is being confined to a very small box.
The spiritual path is to be opened to the **knowing** of
Divine connection and wondering (asking more and more
questions along the way) as you wander on your path
through life. Wandering is not being "lost" but rather just
the opposite--it is moving through life as you ask the real
questions about life and who you are.

To live in a Universe that is always a mystery and
full of unanswerable questions requires of us a greater
responsibility to seek answers but also to know when we
can just admire the Beauty of all we cannot yet
understand from this earthly perspective. Theology

teaches people to be afraid as it closes down the human spirit and reduces it to the very small box of beliefs only. The spiritual path of the seeker however, opens us up to far more than we've ever known as we relax in Divine connection with the Designer of that Universe. This openness is what teaches us to be responsible for how we live, what we seek, how we relate to all others as co-travelers on the way back home, how we create community instead of the "lone ranger" syndrome of independence, how we live in **inter**dependence, and the questions we ask to know our purpose for being here on the planet.

The spiritual path is far more delightful, challenging, interesting, difficult, rewarding, fun, fulfilling, mysterious, and engaging than being in a religious system where we think we have it all figured out. But why would it be more difficult? It is difficult to the extent that we must, in effect, learn a new language. That language is the "silent language" of Spirit that opens deep within our intuitive Self. Humans knew of this long before the alphabet and words were invented and spoken as the main means of communication. The language of Spirit is a Universal communication that speaks to us of wisdom, love, insights, awareness, knowing, understanding, and connection. Humans have called it "intuition" because they knew of no other way to understand it. If we sit with nature long enough, we learn of the presence of Spirit within all parts of creation. However conflicting this is with Western thinking, it is far more real than the Western mind has known.

If I sit with my fellow-pilgrims long enough, I see the same presence in them however masked by the ego or enhanced by remembering who I am and who they are. Nature can teach me much, but my "family" will teach me far more if I open to learning with them. May we choose to be filled with kindness, connection, compassion, sharing, learning together, celebrating, listening, and dancing together in community. We are walking each other home! And, Someone has left the Light on for us. That Light is within and your Divine Self is IT!

Spirituality lives within the mystery and embraces the spiritual path of continual learning, choosing, doubting, wondering, exporting, growing, discerning, listening, and knowing. We have, deep within us, all we need--the power (Light) to choose, to be, to heal, to love, to speak, to transform, to learn, and to grow. You are The Divine in human form.

CHAPTER 5--OR WOULD YOU RATHER BE PAIN FREE?

We've all encountered some "rathers" as we live this present reality that we call life. There are many bumper stickers that reveal the desire to be somewhere else or be doing something else other than what is true in the present moment. "I'd rather be on the beach," "I'd rather be flying," or "I'd rather be anywhere else but here!," are just a few. The real issue is what's missing in our present life situations and why that is our experience. What has gone wrong? Why is this happening to me? Who am I? What is the purpose of all this?

Perhaps it is something like walking in the Arizona desert. There on the plateaus, deep in the valleys, and high on the vast boulders of the mountain range nearby, awaits what I have not yet known as I wander through the cactus and its thorns, a rattlesnake, and a scorpion--the reminders of potential danger but not really a threat. In both the waterless promises of the mirage just ahead and the slippery slope of climbing higher and higher, I see Beauty everywhere on my journey back home.

What are the reasons for feeling dissatisfied? Don't we all face this at times? Are not most of us seeking a "better place;" more happiness (whatever that might mean), more security (however defined), or less difficulties than are on our plate today. "Who are you? Who? Who?" are the words of a song we all know. Then we all change those words at times to "Why am I? Why? Why?"

When we dream of a "rather," we are feeling some kind of dissatisfaction, pain, frustration, anxiety, or discomfort. What is it that we really seek? When the time comes that we then experience the beach, flying, vacation, eating out, or pursuing any favorite activity; who are we then, in that moment? Where ever we go, whatever we do, one issue is our constant reality; we always have to take ourselves along. That means, while I'm in the midst of my favorite activity, I am still me with all my needs--both met and unmet at the same time. This is the nature of life.

The key to all of life is getting our needs met! That is what every action is about and why we make the choices that we do. How we go about meeting our needs is the test of who we are. We can get our needs met by exerting a selfish ego that may look like: violence, denial, dishonest, blame, anger, projection, control of others, and many more--all of which are destructive. We can also choose to get our needs met in loving, connected ways like: compassion, empathy, honest communication, service to others, honoring myself, honoring others, actions compatible with community values, meaningful work or play, and many other ways. All of these positive and productive ways of meeting our needs are necessary in a world where everyone wins. (See my book, *Jesus Was Not a Christian* for more on this)

There is however, another ingredient in getting our needs met that will 1) help us overcome the negative energies of the ego, 2) assist us in a practice of positive and affirmative acts and choices, and 3) provide the energy within to be fully who I've come here to be and to become; and also love you and encourage you to be and become all you've come here to be. That ingredient is the choice to continuously "birth a new self" within (deal with my shadows) and purposely develop deeper qualities of being. (See Volumes IV and VI for more) We must learn to practice these processes with and for each other. All of us as humans are here to do this work. When we can get our needs met in positive and constructive ways, in that process we develop deeper qualities of being, of loving service, and of empathic support for one another. We are more alike than we are different. This birthing process is the call of the Aramaic Jesus--the non-Christian spiritual teacher who has been left out of the English Bible and the doctrines of the church. What he actually taught was far from religious nonsense. He taught the beauty of being spiritual midwives with and for each other, working together to become all we can be as we give birth to that new self continually.

54

We can believe in compassion, in honesty, in love, in harmony, in wholeness, or in whatever qualities we want to be, without yet being the fullest expressions of any of them. What is the difference between believing in the qualities of woodworking, and actually being an accomplished woodworker? What is the difference between believing in the qualities of love, and actually being known as a loving person? The difference is practice. I can only be_____ by a conscious and purposeful practice of that value, that energy, or that quality.

So what does all this have to do with pain and suffering? I must be and become that kind of person right where I am now in this moment, and in this moment, and in the next. I must bloom where I've been planted; just like a tree does each and every day. A tree can't decide to move to a different place in my yard nor in the forest. (The trees in *Lord of the Rings* come to mind for me)The quality of a tree is that it is planted! Spiritually, we too, are planted; in this body, in this family, in these relationships. Yet even as we move about or move away, we take our self along for the journey. The choice remains--do I hold on to what has been or do I become new; learn to choose more wisely, relate more deeply, love more fully, and become more of who I came here to be. The choice is mine, always.

Some trees find themselves growing in the woods. Others sprout in the desert or in someone's back yard. The most productive trees are usually those that have been "planted" by a stream of life- enhancing water. There it is most likely to prosper as a tree is designed to do. The more "life source" a tree takes in, the more it will fully be what it is designed to be. **The same is true with us.** The more we partake of our Source of Life, the more fruit we will bear. If we fail to participate in the spiritual practices that keep us continually experiencing Divine connection deep within, we will not bear ripe fruit. Those practices take us beyond the dogma of religion. By choosing meditation, inner reflection, loving service, unconditional love, helping others get needs met, and much more, we are living in the spiritual practices of Yeshua. Religious activities like traditional prayer, church attendance, worship, false piety, and many more do not make me more loving. In fact, more often than not, those actions can keep me from the deeper spiritual practices and become a hindrance if I stop with the externals of religion and do not choose the internals of spiritual practices. If we fail to continually seek to be the best person we can be, activate compassion, and bring forth empathic service to others in "community," we can expect our leaves to wither and fruit being conspicuous by its absence. What do you choose? One can warm a pew or warm a heart!

To believe in flying doesn't make you a pilot. To believe in love doesn't make you loving. It requires far more than reading the owner's manual in your car for you to become a good driver. Practice, practice, practice, is the old expression that never wears out. I must go **beyond beliefs** in every area of life and **actually practice** what I value until I become that which I desire to be.

We can choose to just exist where we are "planted," or we can choose to be and become far more than we've yet experienced. **We can choose to seek the gifts in pain and suffering and allow them to be guides for our journey through life.** Even here and now in times of discouragement, pain, or struggle, we can choose to become more. In times of delight, celebration, and loving connections, we can choose to become more. We can learn from each moment, each experience, each lesson, and each person in our world. The keys to it all is to live in Divine Connection and practice what we know to be the highest good even if (especially if) it is not easy to do. It is in doing and being my best and highest self in the times of difficulty that reveal who I truly am.

To live in a state of being pain free would be the place where we would not be learning deeper truths as often as we can by listening to what pain and suffering want to teach us. The secret? To look pain and suffering "in the eyes" and say, "Thank you for the insights you are offering me. At this moment, I cannot see our gift, but I will not fail to learn, so show me the reason you are here! Show me what I am missing in this moment. I will not push you away and pretend. Show me. Thank you."

Of course our "thank you" is not directed at the pain and suffering but to The Divine within. This is the key to knowing, claiming, and learning the reason for our experiences of pain and suffering or difficulties. As we open our being to The Divine perspective we are at peace. Then we open our understanding to knowing the gifts. The answers are already within you!

(And, just as I wrote the preceding paragraph, I stopped and practiced this myself. I've been struggling with an issue in my life, so surrendering once again to the Beauty of The Divine within, I experience peace flooding my   heart as I write this. I will know the gifts once again. I've been practicing this principle for many years. It is a practice that I'll never outgrow. I will continue to "walk my talk.")

Without the "shadows" of difficulties as well as the "light" of flowing in beauty of life, there could be no "picture" because all beautiful images on canvas or otherwise, are the products of light and shadow that create the form we love. Pain and suffering are no more than the "shadows" that The Divine uses to help us paint our "picture" more and more beautifully. The light of The

Divine is always ours to know in the midst of all shadows. That is the beauty of living in the spiritual practices of who we truly are.

Don't take the "shadows" so seriously! Love them. Challenge them to reveal their beauty! It is through those who practice this beauty of dancing with both shadow and light that The Divine reveals Its purpose. You are IT! Let us practice these together and dance together in community and delight. WE are IT as we choose **to not be intimidated** by the gifts to be found in difficulties, pain and what we feel as "suffering."

CHAPTER 6--SPIRITUALITY IS MORE THAN RELIGION

Running through a forest blindfolded will not get you very far down a wooded trail that winds through the trees, boulders, logs, and underbrush. Yet that is very much like someone who is trying to discover their personal spiritual path by staying in any man-made religion. Being battered and bruised from running into trees you can't see is like being blindsided by the theological barriers, rules, and belief structures of religious institutions. My writing is not intended to be a criticism of people who are doing the best they can to find and live a meaningful spiritual life. It is, however, a critique of the professional religious hierarchies that are more interested in their own precepts, practices, interpretations, and the applications thereof. The spiritual path is where we can find meaning in life, in pain and suffering like never before, in success, in failure, in our innermost goals and celebrations that come as we live the life we were intended to live. Religion only makes ones path more difficult by creating theological guilt and shame. Then they create some theological "salvation" as the answer to their first distortion. It is theology that is the boulders, logs, swamps, and the underbrush on the human path through the forest of life. Religion creates pain and suffering--it does not alleviate it in any way that is healing for the human spirit.

To write about the human quest for deeper truth that goes far beyond any man-made religion, is to write about the Aramaic Yeshua (Jesus), the one that many in religion call "lord." But by his own words, he is not lord for anyone that is not practicing what he taught. He has been lost in the dust of history and replaced with theology and beliefs about him instead of a practice of what he taught.

No theologian, priest, or minister knows any more about The Divine from a study of theology than you know right now in this moment. No one can know the delights of the finest ice cream on a hot summer day just by reading about it. Until you experience that for yourself, there is no way to know how satisfying it is. A deeper experience with what some call "God" is not at all dependent upon an understanding of man-made theology. Knowledge of The Divine is internal, relational, experiential, and experimental. **It is experimental** because it requires asking, listening, discerning, acting, evaluating, observing the results, and then doing all these practices again and again. The Divine can only be known through the experience that comes to one who learns to *discern* and *know* the "silent voice" and presence of The Divine deep within. That knowledge can only come through testing of the "voices" we hear and **learning by experience** to know which ones are from The Divine and which ones are from our own ego. Getting to that place of deep inner knowing is where one finds the gifts in pain and suffering and much more. It takes longer and requires much more work than just believing. Choosing to let spiritual truth change the way we live is the essence of Yeshua's life and teaching. Personal spiritual practice is far beyond gaining information alone. Reading a flight manual doesn't make you a pilot; just like beliefs without practice only make someone a spectator without the depth of knowing. Experiencing the inner knowing is for those who are neither faint of heart nor looking for the easy road to heaven. And, it requires a determination that is characteristic of one who is pursuing the treasure of a life-time. *What is the most valuable treasure you could find? Why would that hold more value for you than anything else? What need of yours would that treasure meet?*

When Christianity lost Yeshua and his message, its leaders developed an easy theological path instead of the sometimes difficult, inner transformational work that Jesus said was required. All of their theological dogma is built on the premise that we are separate from The Divine and we must face judgment, punishment, or hell. (For proof that there is no "hell" see my book *Jesus Was Not a Christian*). That is **the easy path;** it is not what Jesus taught. Christianity has never, at any time in its history, held a church council that focused on how Christians could be more loving, how they could return kindness to one who has hurt them, how to turn the other cheek, nor how to love one's enemies or how to know the gifts in pain and suffering. Their focus has always been on "correct" beliefs instead. And, of course, they determined what was "correct" and what wasn't.

Yeshua taught of a spiritual path of discovery—of making choices, of practicing love for The Divine, self and others in a way that will require every ounce of strength you can muster and then some, of denying your "self," of taking up your daily cross, of following him by practicing his words, discovering your unique purpose in life through the adventures of pain and suffering and more. There is no convenient end to what is required of you and I on the path Yeshua described. *How do I learn to love my enemies? How do I love my neighbor in the same ways I love myself? How do I practice what I know is right so that my inside and outside match?* After fifty-plus years of not seeing the need to go beyond belief and to actually practice what I claimed to understand, I have been working very hard to make sure my actions match my words. I had no idea that this work would take so long and be so difficult at times. I am still working on this and will be for the rest of my life. This inner work has resulted in tangible experiences with The Divine. Experiences of which I was previously unaware

The spiritual path of Yeshua and the kingdom of heaven within you is about living as the Good Samaritan; turning the other cheek; putting down your sword; learning how to love yourself, your neighbor, and your enemies; becoming peacemakers instead of waging war; feeding the hungry, caring for orphans, widows, and the poor, returning kindness to those who have hurt you; and so much more. Love for all others is to love all parts of The One. And, you are part of that Divine Reality. This kind of love can be embodied by understanding that pain and suffering are just a "wake up call" to help us get our eternal self back on track.

"Every culture has its myths and legends that tell its people how the world they know came into being from a place or a world they do not know. Our own culture has its myths as well, only we are less willing to call them myths. 'Mysteries' suits some people better. For others, 'unsolved problems' is an even more acceptable expression. It is as though there were many veils between the world we know and the one we do not know. Every time we pull away one veil hoping to reveal the answers to our questions, we find only another veil, another question. And yet we continue to seek. What draws us? What makes us believe that there are answers? What possesses us to continue to explore on the boundaries of consciousness, confident that if we probe only a little longer, only a little deeper, we will uncover what we are looking for?" (*Seeing Through The Visible World,* p. 7, June Singer)

The way of religion always requires of us a direct confrontation with the idea of wholeness and/or some kind of perfection. This is not so on the path of spiritual practices. Religion sees an "ideal." Spirituality is about the transformation of shadow and honesty about who we are. Religion pretends. Spirituality steps into the depths of the human experiences--even what is difficult! **Especially what is difficult and not easy to understand at times!**

> "This involves the recognition of the dark side within oneself and in the world, and a willingness to face up to it. The traditional religions, with their litanies of thou-shalt-nots, encourage the repression of the shadow, the part of the self that is unacceptable in terms of collective mores...the integration of the shadow by progressively dealing with the ignorant and destructive parts of one's own nature." (Ibid.)

Do you long for a deeper reality and a peaceful knowing inside yourself that you are connected to The Divine? Do you dare to know that you are part of The Divine? Are you ready to begin that journey in a new way? Are you tired of feeling like a theological victim?

The curse of America, and our materialistic way of life, is that our lives of comfort and ease have required us to pay an extraordinarily high spiritual price. We have become spiritually bankrupt with our SUV's, boats, expensive homes, sports, politics, status, investments, and our list of material possessions. Living in the midst of relative ease, we have little need to look for a deeper truth until tragedy strikes and we are left without something we have valued more than we should have.

> "We do know a great deal about the world that lies just beyond the visible world. But in our daily lives, most of us behave as though we do not know about it or that it does not matter. In exchange for the promise of security, many people put a barrier between themselves and the adventures in consciousness that could put a whole new light on their personal lives and, extrapolated, on the society in which we live." (Ibid.)

What do you most yearn for? Is that what you're experiencing right now? If you knew there was a vast treasure buried beneath you, how hard would you work to find it? If you want an easy spiritual path, put this book down and walk away. If you want to know where to find real connection to The Divine, experiences of deeper love, a profound peace that comes from inner knowing, and the delight of responsible choosing—along with the hard work of personal transformation, you can! If you seek, you will find. The spiritual path of Jesus is not for the faint of heart.

As human beings, perhaps our greatest barrier to Divine Connection is that we put too much stock in what we can see with our eyes. When all of what we see in a physical world becomes more real to us than what we cannot see, it is easy to lose sight of what is most real—*all that we cannot see.* Everything you see with your eyes is temporary and is passing away. Your car has more rust on it today than it did yesterday! All that you cannot see physically is eternal and therefore is the most valuable. ***Have you ever made a list of the realities that you can't see with your eyes?***

> "The decisive question for humans is: Are they related to something infinite or not? That is the telling question of their lives. Only if we know that the thing which truly matters is the infinite can we avoid fixing our interest upon futilities, and upon all kinds of goals which are not of real importance. Thus we demand that the world grant us recognition for qualities which we regard as personal possessions: our talent or our beauty. The more a person lays stress on false possessions, and the less sensitivity he has for what is essential, the less satisfying is his life. He/she feels limited because they have limited aims, and the result is envy and jealousy. If we understand and feel that here in this life we already have a link with the infinite, desires and attitudes change. In the final analysis, we count for something only because of the essential we embody, and if we do not embody that, life is wasted." *Memories, Dreams, Reflections,* by Carl Jung, p. 325 (some words changed for clarity)

Closely related to the problem of seeing is the problem of hearing. *To what are we listening most*? *What are we tuning out by the choice to listen to the voices of our society in a physical world? What are we thus missing?* Praying without listening is like chewing without swallowing. *What voices are the most real for you?* The voices of friends, family, television, music, sports, Wall Street, your very own thoughts, and all other external voices rob us of being able to hear the voice of The Divine. In the Psalms we read, "Be still and know that I am God." This is a requirement that most Americans don't want to hear. Being still and being busy are choices that we make.

Many find it easier to let the spiritual surrogates (clergy) "hear" for them and then reveal what "God has said." Nothing is more dangerous to one's spiritual path than that. No one else can eat for you, drink for you, sleep for you, or exercise for you. You are the only one who can hear The Divine for yourself. Many preachers call that the *"slippery slope"* to danger and destruction. It is, however, the way of Jesus. Each person who wants you to follow them has already made choices for their own path but they do not call their actions a "slippery slope." They are following someone else's examples and choices. What makes their slippery slope better than yours?

When is the last time you took charge of your own spiritual life, asked the questions the clergy can't answer, and set out on a quest to know a deeper truth? Why has the clergy warned us of the dangers of personal exploration? Why have they called that the *"slippery slope"* to hell? Why have we not valued the questioning that leads to deeper discovery, the hunger that leads to a banquet spread before us, or a thirst that takes us to the deeper well? These pages will provide you with more tools for this inner journey to the delights of spiritual-path-discoveries deep within your higher self.

Easy or difficult? Which would you choose? Easy or right? Which holds the most value for you? Of course, the answer you give depends on what you seek. Perhaps nothing costs us more than doing what is easy at the expense of what is right. Easy is the mask that keeps us from knowing with whom we are dancing. Like Mardi Gras in New Orleans, there is more behind the masks than the party is worth.

The deeper quest, the adventure, the exploration, and the choice to do what is most rewarding are the juices of life that flow within one's spirit and make life worth living. They all hold so much more than we have experienced when compared to the boredom of conformity. You can follow a guide through the forest and listen to boring stories of someone else's adventures, *or you can go on your own safari, explore your own path, and make some delightful discoveries instead of just depending upon third-hand information.* There is not just one path through the forest! More dangerous you say? Not at all. When you have "The Guide" within you, all is well, even when you experience doubts, questions, or some pain along the way.

All of us know what pain is like. Pain is our common experience. Examples all around us show people's responses to it. We try to deny it, forget it, cover it up, pretend it's not real or drown it with such things as drugs, alcohol, work, music, sports, church attendance, prayer, food, anger, sex, shopping, or whatever distracts us from it temporarily. But unless pain is transformed within us it will not loosen its grip on our soul, our heart, and our mind. There is a deep purpose for pain and suffering as we learn to claim the gifts in them. To awaken from our "dream" is only one of those gifts.

I carried the pain of physical and mental abuse in my body and soul since I was three years old. The church and its theology provided no answers for that pain. No amount of reading the Bible, praying, singing, or worshipping in church could ever deal with the tremendous pain inside and the torment of not ever being good enough that came out of being a victim. Eventually I had to begin my own spiritual path of discovery. The process of adventures and discoveries, later in life, became the source of deep healing for me. Sure, there is more to do, but at the age of sixty-six I have found great relief from the pain of the past. The healing of a painful past doesn't have to take that long. I am writing this series of books to help you find more light for your path of healing too. The past can evolve into love, delight, and purpose far more quickly than it took me to get there. And, my inner work continues. It is my privilege to be able to do the work as long as I am alive here on the planet. *I don't have to do it. I get to do it.* I've discovered that there are some very important benefits from the past pain in my life. I am waking up. I wouldn't trade any of it for the easy path. The easy path would have kept me from the eternal value of learning from the experiences that I now know I agreed to go through before I came to the planet. The Divine is finally real—I know!

Just as the river in the desert only appears after waiting for the rain to fall; much like the flower that awaits its own blooming, or the bud of a new branch eagerly desiring to become much more than it now is, we too await our blooming and the deepest purpose we've yet known. All these and more are there to remind me of my potential as it stirs deep within--awaiting the rainfall of Divine connection. Residing in my every breath as I consciously know that I am more than I've yet become, the reality of The Divine within is opening; opening me to Life!

But why did you come to this planet? Do you remember? You are not just "dust in the wind" of a predatory capitalist society or any society for that matter. You are more than a potential banquet for worms. *Who are you? What is your unique contribution to the planet that no one else can do as well as you can?* Dr. Marshall Rosenberg, author of many "non-violent communication" books, and lecturer on the same, says that our deepest desire and need is making the world more beautiful for others through empathic service to them. He is only reminding us of Jesus' words. His non-violent communication model is the practice of loving of neighbor, self, and enemy.

We have the privilege of serving The Divine by making others' lives more beautiful. All human beings are individual parts of The Divine. *We are one.* We will never fully experience The Divine apart from seeing other people as parts of that Whole. There is only "one planet, one people, and one world for us all." (Doug Bottorff— from his cd, One World) The planet Earth and all its inhabitants await your contribution to the global healing that we so desperately need. Indeed, all creation needs what you and your gifts will contribute. Is there a greater purpose? How can we become more than we are now? Do we really want to be the very best we can be? What is required of us to keep the eternal in perspective? Beyond the temporary world, what do you see?

Let's explore together the path to the spiritual depths of the kingdom of heaven ***inside us*** as Yeshua declared to be the truth. Let's run through the forest together without the blindfolds. Watch carefully. Consciousness is sneaking up on you!

Chapter 7--Forgiveness: Setting Yourself Free

We all know the delights of anticipating Thanksgiving dinner at home or in our favorite restaurant. The wonderful aromas of roasted turkey, the stuffing we can't resist, and the yummy gravy that cascades down the mound of steaming mashed potatoes as it forms enticing puddles around our plate-full of mouth-watering morsels. Add to that your favorite wine, poured and ready to sip.

But wait....what if, after you saw that irresistible array of delicious food, you left the table without eating any of it? Would just believing in the existence of food be enough for you? How could you ever "know" how wonderful food can taste if you never took it in and experienced the abatement of your hunger? Just seeing it, believing in it, and smelling it will never satisfy your needs.

Absurd you say? Indeed it would be. Yet that is exactly what so many people do when they go through the rituals of organized religion's externals: stained glass, memorized repetitions of words, music, preaching, obedience to rules, contrived forgiveness, and the constant reminder of their guilt and the need to "behave"--all without experiencing a real, satisfying, and loving connection with The Divine deep within. Church can be like walking away from the Thanksgiving table without eating the food set before you. Just "beliefs" alone will never satisfy like experience does.

Sometimes our illusions are like the lizard that darts away as it seeks refuge in the landscape that seems to hide it from all that may see. Yet it remains hiding   in an illusion of safety, not knowing that it is still visible and unaware of its vulnerability in what only seems to be safe. Humans too hide in the illusions of the material world--religion, money, jobs, hopes, cars, careers, plans, goals, hopes, and dreams--not understanding that they are never safe in any of those temporary shelters.

Perhaps there are a handful of individuals who do experience a bit of Divine presence within the parade of Christianity's externals, but that path is treacherous. To be required to constantly traverse the landscape of guilt, the eucharist, shame, repentance, forgiveness, and "fabricated grace" is a tragic path that is woefully unnecessary. It also greatly diminishes the healthy self-esteem of who we really are. The constant labeling of people as "sinners" only serves to keep them in the prison of theology, much like the story of The Scarlett Letter. In that story the woman was externally labeled so as to make sure she was imprisoned in the shame forced upon her by the patriarchs in control. (See Volume VII) Shunning others and condemning them is still the pattern today seen when many churches treat our LGBT friends with anger and contempt. How wonderfully loving! Indeed, it would be interesting to see how many televangelists today would have to appear on their shows with a scarlet "A" on the front of their expensive suits.

The distortion-of-externals is the curse of any form of Christianity that is void of practicing Jesus' teachings. Who decided that "God" must be appeased instead of experiencing love and practicing love as Jesus taught? Why have men defined "God" as separate, angry, and eager to punish? Since when does my surrender to patriarchal control mean that I am more pleasing to The Divine? Jesus said that it wasn't that way! Is Divine favor only realized by keeping the rules of men? Who says so and why?

That is, however, exactly what was taught in the ancient nomadic Hebrew culture when 603 laws were invented and labeled as commandments from some god up in heaven. Once the fabricated idea that they were "chosen" and "special" beyond all other people, then keeping the rules became "proof" that they were thus endowed. To not eat pork chops (bacon and ham included) became one of those external validations that "God" was pleased with them. The problem was that another 602 laws and rules were lurking in the minds of the patriarchs that must be obeyed or else! Making sure one doesn't eat gravy, shave his face, eats lobster or shrimp, and live as a gay person were just a few more of the idiotic rules from the professional god experts. **It has never been a "SIN" to do or be any of the above!**

The same hypocritical rules that create pain and suffering, dreamed up by the patriarchs of religion, allowed the people of that day to take slaves from neighboring countries, to sell their daughters into sex slavery, to stone any neighbor who wasn't observing the Sabbath, and to never touch the skin of a dead pig--unless you are playing football?? (see Exodus and Leviticus for details) What was "kosher" for the ancients had zero value when it came to pleasing a fabricated deity. No one is chosen above any other person! Even the Bible says that "God is not a respecter of persons." Or maybe they cut that page out. It is only a dichotomous and dubious faith that leads to the kind of external conformity which requires that some god be pleased. A god that must be appeased by human conformity is not the god that Jesus knew. The real Divine is within. Only with an internal experience of Divinity can we ever know the gifts that pain and suffering want to bring to us.

Who says that the Creator, the Source of life, and the One who is the essence of Love, requires strict obedience to fabricated rules in order to be pleased? I'm thinking that the Sovereign of the Universe has more important things to do. Why would the Creator be angry with what "he" had created? **It was men who decided that if the humans were to choose for themselves, it would be "sin" and wickedness to do so.** Nothing has created more pain and suffering than this. "Sin" is the worst kind of pain and torment. It is totally unnecessary and instead of helping us see clearly, it only covers over the truth about how beautiful we really are. The gift that awaits us through pain and suffering is first to walk free of religion and then step into who you truly chose to be when you came to the planet.

There were no rules in the Garden of Eden--it is only the English Bible that makes the case for "sin" beginning there. There is no mention of "sin" in that story! There was no sin in the actions of Adam and Eve--just free choice. The "Garden of Eden" story didn't really happen anyway. It is a story told to convey truth. That is the magic of myth. A myth is intended to emphasize and teach truth, even though it is just a story. Story is one of the most powerful teaching tools we know. The truth conveyed is the point. Jesus' parables did not really happen either. He told stories to reveal truth and he did so repeatedly. Free choice is always a sin in the minds of control-focused men who need to have people obey them in order to feel good.

In order that the first humans might experience what it means to be fully alive, to choose, and to understand the results of their choices, whether good or ill, they needed to experience life beyond the robot-like existence of a "perfect environment of innocence." What is innocence anyway? If there are no rules, who then can be guilty of anything? It requires rules in order to condemn people for breaking them. To give someone choice and then severely punish her/him for choosing, is not the nature of The Divine that Jesus knew. It would have been really stupid and mean of "God" to put a tree in the garden, to then speak about choosing, and then make it impossible for them to choose without severe and eternal consequences.

The "evil" of choosing for oneself is only a projection of the patriarchal mind. There was no punitive warning to Adam and Eve--just a choice between two paths. The words "thou shalt surely die" was not punishment but the ultimate result of knowing good and evil by experience. To discover the gifts in all our pain is just one of the results of choosing. To choose the path of knowing the difference between "good and evil" would mean the human experience of death would also be part of the choice. How else could it be? Death was not punishment. Death is not the end of the human--it is only the end of this one lifetime. There is no fear in death for the ones who know that the human spirit is part of The Divine and cannot be destroyed.

Divinity is a continuum of life. Had their choice been as heinous as the patriarchs made it to be, then "God" would have made them into a human sacrifice and torched them or some animal on an altar just like they later claimed was required for all human "sinning." But then, more humans would have been required on the scene. God did not torch them! And, choosing to know the difference between "good" and that which isn't, did not suddenly render their genitals as sinful and needing to be covered. It only opened the door to the most beautiful aspect of being human--choice! Choosing again and again is our destiny. Was it suddenly sinful to be seen without "clothes"; whatever "clothing" might be! If so, then God would be the only one sinning by looking upon them. No one else existed. The word naked in the text does not mean to be without clothes. It has more to do with transparency. If the penis was now to be seen as sinful, why then did the patriarchs later decide that a circumcised penis was required for a man to please God? Was it the foreskin that was so "sinful?" It seems to me, if that were true, "God" would have been telling Adam to improve upon what "he" had just created, and cut off what shouldn't really have been there! What indeed was all that phallus-focus about? After circumcision, did the men walk around with their pants down to prove their devotion to God? How else would anyone know if they were dedicated or not? Since women didn't have a foreskin to offer, I guess they just weren't that important to the patriarch's "god." (See Volume VIII of this series)

Religion is always about externals--like looking at Thanksgiving dinner and then walking away without eating any of it. Spirituality is about internals--like taking in nourishing truths and by that experiencing Divine connection deep within. Choosing what to eat and what not to eat is our heritage. Dessert anyone? Jesus called the Pharisees hypocrites because, in their keeping the rules of religion, the external observance of their laws, they became nothing more than self-righteousness. They wanted "to be seen of men." He told them that they were "full of dead men's bones" because, in all their keeping of rules, they knew zero about The Divine within.

In religion we find greater proof of absolutely zero connection with The Divine energies of love, compassion, healing, and empathic service to others. Externals are about doing. Internals are about being. Keeping external rules is about doing. Working hard at self-denial, acquiescing to the forced observance of religious ideals, and keeping a list for the sake of self-righteousness, are the results of a focus on the self as being bad or "evil", and a god who is punitive at best.

Doing or being? Forced rules or learning by experience? Robotics or choosing wisely? Which most aligns with your spirit? You know that you are much more than a pawn in the hand of religion. You know that you have value beyond what you've been told. We know that religion takes away your divinity and robs you of real, personal experience of Divine connection deep within. We know that compliance is not the nature of The Divine, nor is it required. Divine connection is **union with,** it is **cooperation and alignment** with Divine values, it is **love beyond any other experience,** it is a **flowing with,** it is **choice always,** it is **community** wherein we love and serve others, it is **knowing you are Divine** by nature--the kingdom of heaven is within you--and the Self is good, rather than shameful. Yes, of course, we all have shadow stuff to trans-form--and we can learn to do that transformative work in ourselves first and then do it together. (See Volume VI) We are called by the Aramaic Jesus (Yeshua) to birth a new self continually. We are thus called to become spiritual midwives for each other's birthing of our most magnificent self; the self that we've been hiding behind the shame that was dumped on us by the shadow-masculine that demands control. It takes a great deal of love to do this work effectively. This is one of the most important reasons for building an effective, honoring, and loving community.

Yes, we can! We don't **"have to"** do the inner work. We **"get to"** participate in Divine connection, choose again and again, and learn to make better and better choices. Jesus was always about choice, learning by experience, compassionate service, and growing in our experience of The Divine within! The real "God" is not about rules, but rather desires that we walk in mercy (see all others as equals), in loving kindness (practice justice in all our relationships),   and the delights of walking humbly with the Source of our Life. In this way, our choices and actions reflect oneness with The Divine, not the slavery of conformity to the rules of men that come out of fabricated theology.

There are times that we are aware of an uncertain "risk" that we face in our quest for The Divine. Embodying the gifts in pain and suffering is one of the most beautiful parts of our journey back home. But that uncertainty merges into an opening, a risk that provides beauty, nourishment, and an aroma, like the flower that knows it is here for far more than just itself, as humans appreciate its magnificent colors, or as the bee or butterfly draws life from its nectar, and its scent drifts over the landscape. All this reminds me that I too am here for much more than selfish desires. I am here to awaken from this three-dimensional dream and experience all that is truly real. Only then can I become the nurturing energy of Divine connection as I touch the lives of others around me.

We can learn to sit down to the table of The Divine and partake of all the delicious possibilities of being part of that Essence. We don't eat just once. Neither are we to experience Divine connection just once. This is a powerful, delightful, and continual spiritual experience. And, it is not all fun and games; but even when there is pain to deal with and learn from, we can do it, because this is the path to higher consciousness and to discovering our purpose for coming to the planet.

So what does forgiveness and letting go of the illusion that someone else is more guilty than I am, have to do with all of this? Simply this--forgiving yourself sets YOU free. No longer can anyone hold any power over you! No one can hold you guilty any longer. Then take a long look at the illusions that plague anyone who has bought into the scam of a loveless religion. (See Volume III of this series) You can experience the end of guilt, shame, and remorse deep inside. What a gift to give oneself. You are The Divine in human form. (See Volume II) and you can KNOW this beyond any doubt.

CHAPTER 8--LIVING BEYOND THE "VICTIM"

That moment when--you suddenly realize that you've been cheated, something has been taken from you that cannot be replaced, a painful experience has just been handed you and there's nothing you can do to change it. Tears welling up, cascading down your cheeks, anger bursts forth accompanied by the awareness that you are in that moment--a victim!

These moments have happened to all of us as we wonder how or why it became an issue in our life. To wrestle with "how" and "why" is what we'd all like to avoid. But to try to run away from it is futile whether it takes us years or a few hours. The only way through this is to transform it into what serves us deep inside.

I've been down both roads; the longest of which was a 16 year "dark night of the soul" that seemed it would never end. Why did he do that to me? I wrestled with that until I lost my own self along the way of trying to forget. The gift in it? I choked at the very thought of that. How could there be a gift in all that pain, misery and anguish? But yes, there was a gift--one that would help me awaken and change the course of my life. Now, thirty-six years later I look back with gratitude for the pain and suffering that opened the door to first establishing my own business and later to writing so I could help others heal and awaken too! It was to be a powerful gift that I could never have seen while going through it.

Then there are those "victim" events that happen, not because someone has hurt us out of their own issues, but there was some reason that we allowed them   to take advantage of us without saying "No!" Many times this situation is more painful than the others, when we feel guilt or shame for not standing up to others or worse, feeling that we were not "good enough" or strong enough to take that stand which required them to stop their efforts to victimize us.

Most of us have spent what seems like more than our share of time crying in secret perhaps mostly because we didn't know why we weren't strong enough to stop that situation. Then we cry even more realizing that we may not be able to stop the next one either.

Why do we allow ourselves to be hurt? What happened to us in the past that rendered us so weak? But then is it weakness or is it that we haven't yet learned to "stand our ground" in the face of a would-be-victim-maker? This is why I've written this series of books. I've learned to overcome these issues. You can too if you want to learn how you can.

But then, there is another "victim" situation that is extremely difficult to overcome because in one's blindness to reality, greed in the moment, callous disregard for others, a focus on what feels good, unconscious choices, or a commitment to personal gain. What do these energies have to do with being a victim? It is when we do not see or understand how our own choices can set us up to become a victim that we are in jeopardy in the energies of our illusions. Those illusions contribute to pain and suffering when we do not understand the consequences of our choices, actions, or blind spots and the circumstances that we do not want to change. Therein we are victims because of our own self and the choices that temporarily feel good. But sometimes we do not want to change because of a short-sighted perspective that opens us to the "victim" scenario.

(Example: Recently an open-carry gun enthusiast who was openly carrying a very expensive gun for all to see, was robbed by two other open-carry enthusiasts who wanted his more expensive gun.)

Sometimes ignorance and/or being hell-bent on getting our own way is what sets us up for pain and/or suffering and becoming self-made victims because of the consequences we haven't foreseen. In all of this it can be our ego that gets us into the most trouble. It claims to know the way but it becomes the cause--not the cure.

But what about self-punishment? There is nothing quite as destructive as self-punishment that one carries because somewhere along the way a they came to believe that they deserved to be punished. To live in a way that is contrary to who they truly are--their "real self"--is to invite pain and suffering and feed the victim instead of transforming it.

So often it is one's "faith" that teaches them that they deserve pain and suffering. Any faith that creates that situation with their dogma is more of the illusion than any focus on reality. Faith is no more than "beliefs' without knowing, while still living in the fear that there is more lurking around the next corner. This series of books will help guide anyone away from "faith and fear" and into the beauty of knowing who they are. And with that, they can dance through pain and suffering to the awaiting gifts and celebrate awakening to The Divine within reality. (See www.thedivineiswithinus.com)

If ease and comfort were to continue uninterrupted, would we ever desire to learn of deeper realities? No! We would be too satisfied to change anything and just live on in a state of blindness to any deeper reality.

Without pain and suffering no one would ever try to remember from where they have come and why they are here. Pain and suffering are prods to remember and to awaken, and to live as being fully alive. We are not destined to live forever in delusion! Sometimes we are pre-occupied with being the person we only think that we are. Our task is to gather all the lost parts of our true Self and become acquainted with who we really are and came here to be. The Divine always holds out to us the invitation to find our lost parts and return to our Divine Self that is within--Yeshua called it "the kingdom of heaven within."

Self-realization and self-knowing come only as we gain power over the physical realm of bodies, cars, jobs, homes, and other possessions. It is through pain and suffering that we can see the "temporary" in a new light and choose to define ourselves by what is eternal, conscious, transcendent, and immortal. To discover ones Divine nature and live from that is the greatest delight possible as we overcome the futility of this three-dimensional world. Being and living as "one with The Divine" is the highest good for humanity. Yeshua called that "entering the kingdom that is already within" us. (See Volume VI)

To change the heart of what we are conscious, of what we perceive, of how we relate, of what we treasure, and of what we either hold onto or let go, makes all the difference. Your highest Self is awaiting your discovery, your invitation to take center stage and you choices to never live small again. This way of living in the mastery of overcoming the fear of life and the fear of death!

In all of our spiritual journey we must focus on dealing with dualities. We've been lied to! We've been told of separations between The Divine and humans, men and women, races, religions, nations, and more. The only problem bigger than this is that we've believed the lies of religion, politics, the racists, and the super-rich. In believing those lies we are victims! We must learn to put all the pieces back together--perhaps the greatest challenge for humanity. Before we can ever see that happen we must first put our own self back together; claim those lost parts, focus on who we truly are and live that truth every day. There is no greater "evil" on the planet than the results of teaching separation and believing the lies of it.

One of the most difficult issues we have to deal with is the frustrations of this three-dimensional world wherein what is most "real" for most of the people is the physical things they see, feel, hear, smell, or taste. Our addictions to the sensory perceptions around us is our greatest challenge to overcome. (See Volume I of this series)

"There is no coming to consciousness without pain. People
will do anything, no matter how absurd, in order to avoid

facing their own soul. One does not become enlightened by
imagining figures of light, but by making the darkness
conscious."--C. J. Jung

In consciousness we know that while living in the midst of the chaos of separation, I can choose to be as solid as a huge boulder on the landscape of human struggle. I am not just a part of this physical world, I AM Spirit in a temporary physical body for a short time.

Remembering

The deepest spiritual writers over time have all written of the same deeper issues--that no separation is real, no need to substitute externals for internals, the power and necessity of love, the value of the individual spiritual path, no punishment for anyone, karmic responsibility, and the power of choosing and remembering.

But remember what? Why remembering? Yet, once we learn to see through the illusions of all that is temporary, we begin to "know" something more. Is that remembering? Once we experience the deeper connection with The Divine in meditation, service, loving self and others, letting go of our attachments, waking up, celebrating our mistakes, living beyond victimhood, forgiveness and more, something happens for us. We begin to live the "we" instead of the "me" and therein consciousness rises to a whole new level as remembering takes on a whole "new" resonance with Universal truths. (See Volume III and IV)

But there is another piece of this puzzle. What if remembering were understood as a re-membering; that is to put our own "members" back together. A play on words? Yes, but therein is a powerful insight for the spiritual traveler. How do you see yourself? As the average person, that isn't very important? Who do you, deep inside, believe yourself to be? What are those members of yourself that you've not been including?

The ancient texts speak of an "I-ness," that is a sense of being an individual that is here to remember **and** re-member! Becoming aware of this and practicing it always takes us to the sense of community which is a consciousness beyond the self as being here alone. We are meant to know both I and we!

Before we can embrace the "we," it is required of us that the "I" is remembered and reassembled. It is the bringing together of our parts that have been fractioned or split or broken apart by not remembering. On the stage of our own "play" **we get to create the drama, the dreams, the dialogue, and the dance.** By doing this we can put the parts of our self back together. Those parts are: body, mind, soul, memories, actions, choices, values, hopes, and so much more. Others are watching but it is our play that we get to create. Only you can look within and remember what parts of you are missing, which parts your need to complete your most beautiful self, and how you choose to shine as a Light in the world. Gathering all of your "lost" parts and integrating them into your shining is the work of this lifetime. You can do it! Our lives are so often the drama of remembering and forgetting. From a song of that title comes the words:

> Sometimes I feel the Spirit, Sometimes I feel so
> sad. Sometimes I feel so near it, Other times I hurt
> so bad!

> Some days it all feels wonderful, Some nights I just
> want to cry.

> Sometimes I feel that my dreams can come true
> Sometimes I just want to let them die
> Remembering and forgetting That's the game that
> we play, We drift so far we forget who we really
> are, 'til we remember that love is the way.

> --*Remembering and Forgetting,*

> from the cd by Stephen Fiske,
> Awakening Heart Productions

The seductive power of "what if I choose" is the power of re-membering. As you build the "house" of your being, you create the rooms, the doors, the windows, the art, the table for the feasts to come. This is the Dance of Sacred Wisdom wherein the old splintered self gets to be reassembled as we find the lost parts of ourselves and put them back together by choosing to be a new and different person. You are the script, the dance, and the music of your personal play on the stage of life. You are the producer, the director, and the main actor. Who is it that you have not yet become?

The Prodigal Son

Yeshua told a story (Luke 15:11-32) about forgetting and remembering as one of his parables about the kingdom of heaven within. It is not a true story. It is a parable, which is like a myth, in that it is told to reveal truth rather than being an actual story of real people. Prodigal does not mean wicked, lost, sinful, shameful, immoral, or disdainful as I was always told in church. The church says it means a waster, a squanderer, or one who fritters away what is valuable, an extravagant fool, and one who is unconscious in a sad way. But once again the church is dead wrong.

Proof that this is not a parable about sin/redemption theology is the fact that the son began his journey at home with his family. He is not the picture of one who enters the world as one who is lost, wicked, and separated from The Divine. We all began our journey in the presence of The Divine Mother/Father. It is back to that Presence we are returning; hopefully having learned what we came here to learn.

This story is not just about squandered money but about unconscious living wherein one allows a self-focus to value all that is but temporary. This results in a misuse of their most valuable inner gifts or talents. When will we finally understand the difference between internals and externals and how they affect us? It is a story of "missing the mark" of Divine perfection—not about "sin" which the church describes as wickedness or evil. This is about waking up and remembering.

There is far more involved in this story than what is apparent in the words of text. As Joseph Campbell says: "The familiar life horizon has been outgrown: the old concepts, ideals, and emotional patterns no longer fit; the time for the passing of a threshold is at hand."--*The Hero With a Thousand Faces*, p. 58

> "At the end of childhood, we are called to move out of immaturity into responsibility. If we do not make this passage, if we attach ourselves to our childhood home as a mollusk does to a sea rock, we do not mature. This much is obvious. But what is not so obvious is what *home* means to each of us, when we need to leave it, and how. --*The Feminine Face of God*, p. 45

Leaving home (vs. 12-13) is absolutely essential for anyone who desires to embark upon the spiritual journey of discovering who they are. All of us are called to this adventure. If we are ever going to find our true self and the kingdom within, we must leave behind all that would distract us from our destiny. All that we have "learned" must be challenged with what is unknown. This is the spiritual path. Certainty (as we have known it) must be replaced with what challenges us to see beyond the visible world. How many people stay at home like the elder son and learn very little of that which holds deeper spiritual value?

> "...not just once, at the end of childhood, but many times throughout a lifetime, whenever old certainties need to be released, or perhaps abandoned entirely, so that we can take that enormous step across the threshold of our old home!" Ibid.

To awaken to spiritual realities, to "grow up" spiritually, or to become conscious (vs. 17-18) are required for all of us who are on the spiritual path that Jesus required when he told people that they must "sell all they had," leave home and family behind, and "follow me." The selling and the leaving were not necessarily literal. One does not have to necessarily sell every possession, but rather let go of their value and one's ego attachments to them. It actually may be easier for some to literally sell everything than it would be for them to really let go of the meanings attached to them. One can enter the spiritual path without literally leaving home, but the challenges of doing it that way are sometimes more difficult. "Home" is too often a distraction from seeking spiritual realities that are beyond this realm. As has been said, a ship is safe in the harbor, but is that what ships are for? When are you safe? When do you long for the open sea of learning and discovery?

> "What is left is a consciousness that once felt secure, had categories to fit things into, and knew who it was, where it was going, and why. And what replaces this sureness is 'not knowing.' And openness. And something unspeakably, and sometimes almost unbearably, new." Ibid. p. 48

Money and sex are probably the two most tempting distractions in all of life. The ego uses both to enable blindness. The "out-of-control" ego must find the path to remembering. The prodigal son explored, came to the end of himself, changed from an ego driven life that led him to ruin (as it always will) and remembered, returned, and reconnected with his inner self.

To be "in need" (vs. 16) is the realization that something is missing in one's life—the former answers are no longer answers and the search for more must begin. The search for more is always a returning to "home" but now with a consciousness that has changed me *inside* and the way I used to see "home." My ego is no longer in charge--and this changes everything. There is nothing quite like the ego having to dine with the pigs for it to be seen as that which must be transformed. The ego must be replaced with Spirit—a process that doesn't happen quickly or easily. To pretend that all my "sins" are forgiven is much easier than to actually own my failures, learn from them, and then choose to step into a new way of living and being.

This son neither found "God" up in the sky nor repented in fear of punishment. He "came to his senses." He found himself. He went within himself to discover what had been happening. The "kingdom within" was his new point of reference. The ego always leads to the death of the sacred. "Back home" means to be back in touch with **and to remember** what is real—The Divine within me! This parable is about that "kingdom within" and how to know that! This is what an ego-blindness keeps me from seeing. The ego is blind to the sometimes tragic behavior I use to meet inner needs. A "god" in heaven doesn't help. The Divine within is the power to change.

> "After he spends his inheritance, the "wild" son finds himself at rock bottom, sitting with the pigs. When he turns and lets' go of all that he thought he was, including his pride, he is forgiven and welcomed home again. But at that point, the "good" son, the one who stayed home and took care of business, reacts angrily to his father's welcome feast for his returned brother. This mirrors what happens when an exiled part of our psyche is welcomed back: the whole inner family has to realign itself."--Neil Douglas-Klotz, *The Hidden Gospel*, p. 127

The return--(vs. 22-24) "But the father said to his slaves, 'Quickly bring out the best robe and put it on him and put a ring on his hand and sandals on his feet; and bring the fattened calf, kill it, and let us eat and be merry; for this son of mine was dead, and has come to life again; he was lost, and has been found.' And they began to be merry."

Here is the feminine face of God in action. This is not typically a masculine response. It would be more honest if the mother was given credit for the welcome and the table spread for celebration. There is no talk here of punishment, shame, scolding or rebuke—just the celebration of transformation. Here again is the God that Jesus knew. *He spoke of the "queendom" where no one was excluded from the healing of shadow parts. All is One.* The problem here is that we just aren't told enough about the "prodigal son's" process of transformation. What had he learned? What was new? What would be different than before? What had pain and suffering taught him? The previous abundance he had known never taught him anything except that it was ultimately not important. Any abundance experienced after transformation is always shared, not hoarded.

This son was an example for all of us leaving our heavenly home, coming to the planet to be incarnated in a physical body, living out of the ego, and coming to awareness (remembering) of what is real. It is in the process of transforming our shadow parts, that we return to consciousness and connection with The Divine—our true home. Then the celebration can begin. To awaken is to celebrate.

The truth is, we just don't realize all of who we are and how all of our inner parts are related. The Aramaic reveals this in a vivid way. It goes something like an experience I had recently in the Arizona desert. Almost swept away by the sheer delights of the desert storm as it echoes through the mountains and valleys like the human shadow that some fear; I know that I can yet discover more of my shadow holds the essence of life-giving rainfall for those who welcome both shadow and light. The shadow and the gifts it holds are worth seeking and finding. I see the beauty in embracing the storm, choosing to learn from it, and awaiting the gifts it has to offer. May I awaken to what is real--before I pass from living here in the midst of what is passing away.

The day came when I had to leave Fisher, Illinois— my childhood home. Although my story differs from the prodigal son (as all our stories do) there are some similarities of course. Leaving home was both difficult and not so difficult   at the same time. Leaving to embark on my spiritual journey as a young man was absolutely necessary. Leaving the pain behind was easy. Carrying the memories of it and the shadow it had created inside me were the parts that would require decades of a spiritual journey for me to transform and heal. What I didn't realize was that I had learned by experience what the dark-side shadow masculine is like. At that time it was outside of me. The shadow masculine was in my father and most of the men in the church and the local community. But it was also inside of me as a long dark shadow that I could not see. I'm still working on that transformation process. I've made great progress. I am not the man I was 50 years ago, 5 years ago, nor 6 months ago. There will always be more work to do. The inner work is never fully complete in this life.

I've shared with you, parts of my human drama; not to focus on me, but hopefully to share what may be helpful to you on your spiritual journey. You need to know that I've not just written out of some theory or idealized belief. I've walked the path too. I have nothing of value to share unless I am walking my talk. It is the energy of integrity that I've asked might permeate all that I write or speak. I don't claim to be ahead of anyone. We are all on the spiritual path where we continually learn from each other.

We are all at times, victims of ignorance, of our own choices, of illusions, and of "forgetting." What is the price of remembering? Actually the price is only the loss of an old focus on pleasure, possessions, status in life, reputation, money, and even power over others. But that cost is not easy to pay. The loss of the old can be traumatic but nothing can come close to the intoxicating delights of Divine connection and the beauty of a new way of being. The unreal hides the real. We are here to remember! There is nothing quite like pain and suffering to help us wake up from delusion and ignorance to seeing and knowing and remember who we truly are as we walk that path into conscious connection with our true Self and The Divine within.

> "The most beautiful people I have known are those who have known defeat, known suffering, known struggle, known loss and have fought their way out of the depths. These persons have an understanding of life that fills them with compassion, gentleness, and deep loving concern. Beautiful people do not just happen."--Awareness

CHAPTER 9--LIVING IN GRATITUDE

Finding ourselves existing in a three dimensional world that we inherently know is only temporary, we also realize that we too are here temporarily. How could life be so short? Why? What is behind the veil of this reality? Perhaps that veil is in our own minds and hearts. If so, how are we to transcend the temporary and learn **to live in it and beyond it at the same time?** Not only is this possible, but living in that reality 24/7 can be our ever-present experience.

In this three-dimensional reality humans are faced with choices. How are we to cope with the fear of not surviving? Is this beyond our control? What does that mean? We realize that we are temporarily here but for how long we don't know. Inherent in this lifetime is the fear of losing. As Yoda from Star Wars said: "The fear of losing is the path to the dark side." But lose what? Love? Control? Freedom? Possessions? Why does losing something need to affect our inner security? Actually, it doesn't have to. What if we could lose all fear, insecurities, and needless drama?

Most people, especially men it seems, desperately need to control situations, people, circumstances and the outcomes thereof or they just can't tolerate being alive. But why? Since when does thinking we control something or someone   make us more secure? Fear is the illusion that creates greed, lust for power, and attachments to the material world. The proof of that is seen in the illusion of separation and the need to continue to control others or else life just isn't worth living. Perpetual control comes out of one's deepest fears and insecurities. The "need" to control is greatest evidence that such a person has zero connection with The Divine.

Standing firm in the energies of Divine connection and unconditional love like the tree amidst the desert storm, I too can be strengthened by each blowing of the wind and the rain that encompasses me. Yet the tree remains as the most beautiful provider of shade for all who need it. I am reminded of the beauty of pain and suffering which yields its gifts to me as I understand that I too, am here on the planet to be shade for others on their human journey.

What does it mean to "not have enough?" Enough what?--time, food, money, security, possessions? What does enough mean? How do we know what enough looks like? If you died tomorrow, would what you have today be enough? The truth is we don't even know what "enough" means! If we could step into a whole new realm of consciousness that transcended all we don't know, would we do that? What if we were to find our definitions of reality transformed into a state of never again worrying about any "need?" Would we do what is required of us to live in that reality? How difficult is it to let go? Letting go of our illusions actually may not be that difficult! Interested? You are about to discover how.

There is a quality of life that is beyond being out-of-control or needing to control. There is a reality beyond all competitions. Why do we need to compete? Isn't that about the fear of losing? Maybe all competition is nothing but the fear of losing. What if there were greater gifts in "losing" than there are in winning? There can be! And, I don't mean feeling that you are a loser or believing the lies that were told to you like, "you deserve the worst" or "you're not good enough to win!" Those lies come from people who are projecting some hidden energy or agenda onto us! Like the person who saw their mother or father completely diminished by a spouse and they consciously or unconsciously want to be sure that you pay the price for their pain.

So what does all that have to do with gratitude? Gratitude is a conscious step out of feeling the energy of lack or a focus on what we don't have. To pray is always a focus on what is missing in your life. Isn't prayer usually asking for more because of "needing" something want but don't have? Prayer is a focus on needs instead of answers. The only prayer that is needed is "Thank You"! Thank you is the energy of gratitude. Thank you is opening the doors to receive. Thank you and gratitude are the same. Thank you is the recognition that I cannot make things happen by myself. I need help. How do I get that help? Gratitude is connection to the power that can open the doors "with" me. Gratitude is Divine connection. Gratitude is surrender within connection. **Surrender does not mean giving up or being a victim!** Surrender is to flow together with and in connection with my Higher Self which is The Divine Within. TOGETHER we will accomplish far more than going it alone. Together we will solve the problems we face. Together we will flow in the beauty of needs being met and then share with others as we **create a world where everyone wins.** A winner is not the one who gains at the expense of someone else. A true winner is one who wins **along with others**. Together we are all winners. Separated we are all losers.

Practicing gratitude then becomes living in the sheer delight of serendipity and "Divine magic" where unexpected things happen right before our eyes, problems are solved, doors are opened, needs are met, and our hearts overflow with delight inexpressible. Gratitude takes us into beauty as never before. Delight and appreciation become our "mantras."

People who are living in gratitude meet each other in cooperation, appreciation, and community. We connect with each other in the celebration of life. We share each other's purpose for being alive here on the planet. Then all of our connections break forth into creativity. Creativity yields more and more opportunity for others to find their purpose in life and return the energies of gratitude, connection, delight and a growing community.

In all of our experiences we can learn to live in a three dimensional world but are no longer attached to the things that are in it. We exist beyond the material as we dwell in the spiritual realms. Yet we learn to integrate both in cosmic connections. What we truly experience in all of this is that we are living "eternal life" right NOW! We've always been eternal. Our temporary time in this reality is part of our eternal progress whereby we will serve Divine purposes in the ages to come because of what we've learned here and now! Perhaps you'll be someone's guardian angel later on, an E.T., or a spirit guide for a lost soul. The possibilities are endless because you are eternal. Gratitude is the beginning of a grand adventure. Will you take the next step into gratitude, Divine connection, purpose and more? Gratitude replaces fear with a deep delight that carries us past the old patterns.

I write all this out of personal experience--not theory. As I've learned to practice gratitude, my life has taken on a glow of delight that all my friends recognize. I am deeply excited about all that is coming into my life. Your life can reflect this too.

At times, we are all victims of ignorance, of our own choices, of illusions, and of "forgetting." What is the price of remembering? Actually the price is only the loss of an old focus on pleasure, possessions, status in life, reputation, money, and even power over others. But that cost is not easy to pay. The loss of the old can be traumatic but nothing can come close to the intoxicating delights of Divine connection and the beauty of a new way of being. The unreal hides the real. We are here to remember! There is nothing quite like pain and suffering to help us wake up from delusion and ignorance to seeing and knowing and remember who we truly are as we walk that path into conscious connection with our true Self and The Divine within.

As long as I have breath, I will do my best to help others see through the illusions of this temporary planet and choose to see what is far more real. No one can build a portfolio large enough that it cannot be shaken or taken away. But such is the deception of the ones who stake their lives on what is passing away. Many times it is in the vanishing of the temporary that one begins to awaken for the first time.

CHAPTER 10--THE GIFT

A gift in pain and suffering? Absolutely! Allowing yourself to drift into reflecting on this possibility is the key. Opening your mind to what can be, refusing to let your past experiences dictate what your future will be, and choosing to activate a new sense of reality so that beauty and celebration come to you easily, are all required.

> "When adverse events happen in your life, and they most certainly will, do not curse them for they are blessings in disguise. They are the elements you have created in your life. They are to be used as your guides to move you away from that which you dislike; towards that which you love."--Clint G. Bridges, *Spirit Wisdom for Daily Living*, p.77

The challenge before you is the see pain and suffering in a different light than ever before. Instead of avoiding it at all cost and desperately trying pushing it away, you can begin an adventure you've never before encountered, gain new insights from all your experiences and begin to transform all the negatives that you've up-to-now sought to avoid. Many times we'd rather focus on what helps us avoid looking the pain or suffering "in the eyes" and asking for the gift it holds. What we do to insulate ourselves from our experience is the main issue. Seeking more money, a vacation in the Caribbean, a new car, a new boat, a better job or a host of other external things never, ever help us overcome anything. These just push further away the possibility of finding the gift in what is happening.

Attachments are all the things that keeps us "stuck" in a place of being far smaller than we are destined to be. As we give birth to a new self, we are free from all that holds us back; from all that blocks us from the freedom of Being more than we've yet known. To own something and yet not allow it to own me, is the key to seeing what is real and the things which only distract me from knowing that deep inside.

Those kinds of externals are only the gifts that come to us from a predatory capitalist system that teaches us that "things" are the most important part of life. Externals only blind us to what is more real than our everyday issues in this brief and temporary existence here on the planet.

Being taught by religion that we do not deserve to be pain free or suffering free, we grow up thinking that there are no deeper truths to seek, and that trying to find them is only some form of rebellion. For religion there are no deeper truths to know other than what they teach--so shut up, listen and do not stray from the path!

So often we've heard about speaking positive affirmations aloud to somehow manifest something we want to see come about for us. A few years ago I know someone who regularly each day spoke out many affirmations. Yet what I couldn't understand is why she kept speaking these without changing the circumstances in her life that just might help her realize these situations she dreamed of having real in her life. Over and over again she spoke out the same words without doing anything within herself to align her inner self with what she wanted. The truth is, just speaking affirmations won't manifest anything without changing our inner self and seeing if their might be something that is preventing our experiencing what we desire. Affirmations alone will not help us discover the gifts in pain or suffering just by speaking out something that is the opposite of the pain being experienced.

So just how are we to approach pain and suffering in a way that we can open the door to the gifts they hold? We must change the way we ask the question? The question usually asked is the question of a victim--"Why did this happen TO ME?" Or, "Why is this happening TO ME?" Instead, when we ask with curiosity, "Why DID this happen for me?" or "Why IS this happening for me?" everything changes.

The circumstances you face didn't just happen randomly! You've helped create the pain and suffering that you face. They are not some cosmic mistake! Never!

As Barbara Streisand sings: "Just like the seasons, there are reasons for the path we take." How true! We were born to come here and learn from all that we experience. Your life is not a random happening! You chose to be here. You chose what you would come to learn. As Doug Bottorff sings: "High above the earth, I was given birth in love." Why did you choose this path? Why did you choose this family, that place of birth, those circumstances into which you were born?

Stop right now, and gently go deep inside. Breathe deeply and just let yourself ask this: What is the gift for me in my present circumstances? Then you can go further and ask more questions. What is behind all that I see? What Divine purpose is awaiting my understanding? Beyond this lifetime, what am I here to learn and be prepared for? How can I see through this visible world? What have I failed to understand about this temporary reality? What have I allowed to distract me from what is deeper and more important? What is it The Divine is trying to tell me?

Then after asking, just stay aware of everything you hear, see, notice, think, in what is all around you. You may hear something said by someone, on television, in a conversation, see on a sign, notice happening around you and more. Just pay attention and watch for an insight to you question. You will find it. I've done it a thousand times and it always is there. The quiet inner voice of The Divine is waiting for us to get still enough to hear it. It takes practice. Begin today and keep practicing until you find. The nectar of silence is beyond the activities of the mind.

In the gift you discover will be the healing you need from all the pain and suffering. In that gift you will discover a deeper purpose for your life. In that gift you will find reason to celebrate every mistake, grief, and loss. You can step through all you have been into all that you can yet be and know that your life is being transformed by each choice to know the gifts in pain and suffering. Delight awaits you. The more we live in Divine connection the less we will suffer. Pain and suffering are for those who have not been listening. Something must interfere so we will wake up and begin to live. Our transformation of the pain and claiming the gifts in it, awaits us on the other side to doing the inner work.

Some people secretly love pain and suffering because of the attention and self pity they get from it. If that is what they want, that is all they will ever get. How tragic. Pain and suffering ARE NOT the gifts! They only take us to the gifts with the spiritual practices mentioned above. Could it be that pain and suffering are necessary disciplines that remind us to rise above this temporary existence and live in a real connection with The Divine. YES, they are!

When you come to KNOW Divine connection deep inside, you will not mind the drama of the planet so much. You will know that all is well as you stay connected and know that you are The Divine in human form. Knowing and living in your Divinity are the highest gifts ever given to humans. We are One! There is nothing like consciousness of The Divine within that sets us free from all the silly things of this earth. (See Volumes I and II of this series) This knowing relieves us from all the stress in life and sets us upon a path of relief from all the dualities of men and religion in this present existence.

The spiritual person is not the one who spends most of their time in religious activity, but rather in the midst of living life fully, driving to work, cooking the next meal, caring for others in need, shopping for what is needed, shoveling snow, playing golf, or any of a thousand activities, **and is still conscious** of meditation (Divine connection) while sitting or while walking around amidst all the activities of life. Real spirituality is living all of the above while seeing all of life as the quest for spiritual truths and deeper Divine interaction. It is in the middle of all our activities that we can be asking, "What insights can I be gaining right now that will set me free from all that is just temporary?" It is living here and now, yet being in the transcendent energy of awakening that defines "spirituality" and a knowing of Divine connection. This is the Beauty of the eternal joining us in the mundane.

CONCLUSION

It is time to listen to a different voice that has been the old pattern. The old voice of smallness must be replaced with the inner voice of triumph, purpose, living beyond the temporary, of waking up and of dreaming. There is no song that illustrates this quite like the following:

Wake Up & Dream by Ed Tossing & Thom Bishop

Every life is meant for living Every song is to be sung

Every gift is meant for giving It's the same for everyone

For the world was built by dreamers Dreams are real and so it seems

That this world was meant for dreaming If we just wake up and dream

Chorus:

You can wait a lonely lifetime

For a knock upon your door
Ships are safe inside the harbor
But is that what ships are for
All the world was built by dreamers
Dreams are real and so it seems
That this world was meant for dreaming
If we just wake up and dream

I've listened to this song hundreds of times it seems, and I love it more each time I hear it. Let's all wake up and dream!!

My story brought me to see that surrounded by compliance, people who had surrendered to the enslavement of the status quo, and those who'd lost all hope for being more--I refused to be trapped in smallness as I chose the "road less traveled," (from Robert Frost's poem) which, for me, was the road to becoming all I could be. Not knowing what all that might be, I did that knowing that I was not ever trapped. Why? Because I had come to experience the power of choice. The power to choose will always set me free; even flying on the wings of the unknown, choice would lead me to the yet unseen adventures of becoming.

Instead of listening to that old voice, let's listen to another voice--the voice deep within us that tells us the truth about love. The real Jesus did not teach about an angry god somewhere out there. He taught of The Divine Within--the reality for every human being. We are Divine beings, here on the planet and very capable of loving out of that **Source of love that we are.** Love is who we are! Love is what we are! We can choose to learn of our Divinity (not how bad we are) and we can learn to access our Divine Self. Herein is great hope. Herein is the healing we seek and the Love we long to know. Interested? Look at all Ten Volumes of this series and decide what is on your bucket list.

Lightning Source UK Ltd.
Milton Keynes UK
UKOW06f1842200617

303776UK00007B/410/P

9 781541 155572